HOW TO
THINK
ABOUT
MONEY

Jonathan Clements

FOREWORD BY WILLIAM J. BERNSTEIN

ISBN-10: 1523770813
ISBN-13: 978-1523770816

HOW TO THINK
ABOUT MONEY

"In *How to Think About Money*, Jonathan Clements, one of the premier financial writers of our times, provides readers with a roadmap for a successful financial life. It's an easy read that can result in changing the way readers look at investing and life. Read it and reap."

— Mel Lindauer, Forbes.com columnist and co-author of *The Bogleheads' Guide to Investing*

"*How to Think About Money* is financial *feng shui* —a blueprint for harmonizing all the aspects of personal finance into a balanced way of approaching and managing money. Anyone who feels overwhelmed by the challenges of today's world can benefit from Clements's advice on how to make smart financial choices, as well as how to develop, in his words, a 'coherent way to think about their financial life'."

— Janet Bodnar, editor, *Kiplinger's Personal Finance* magazine

"Jonathan Clements writes so well and thinks so clearly that even financial planning, saving, and wise decisions are almost fun to think through with him as our guide."

— Charles Ellis, author of *Winning the Loser's Game*

For Eleanor, Hannah, Henry and Sarah

CONTENTS

ACKNOWLEDGMENTS

In the immortal words of Monty Python's inimitable John Cleese, "And now for something completely different." I hope you will find this to be a personal finance book unlike any other. My goal: to provide readers with a coherent way to think about their financial life, so they worry less about money, make smarter financial choices and squeeze more happiness out of the dollars they have.

There is a second name on the cover, that of William Bernstein. Bill—retired neurologist, money manager and author of a fistful of brilliant books—not only sent me a slew of emails chock-full of ideas for improving *How to Think About Money*, but also wrote to me while on vacation and offered to pen a foreword. He delivered 48 hours later. My apologies to his lovely wife Jane.

I also received great feedback from Nicholas Clements, Charley Ellis, Allan Roth and Mark Sheinkman. As with my *Money Guide*, this book benefited from the copyediting of Prudence Crowther, the cover and interior were designed by David Glaubke, and much of the angst was borne by sweet Lucinda. Many thanks to all of you.

As I wrote this book, I had in mind my children and stepchildren: Eleanor, Hannah, Henry and Sarah. How would I want them to think about their money? I don't claim to have all the answers (and, if I did, they would quickly put me straight). Nonetheless, this is my roadmap for a successful financial life—and it's dedicated to the four of you.

FOREWORD

William J. Bernstein

A uthors usually request book forewords as a favor from a friend or colleague, but this one happened differently. Jonathan didn't ask; rather, he simply requested that I review an early draft of *How to Think About Money*. It so captured the essence of a healthy financial life that I specifically requested the honor.

My sage, sainted mother used to say, "Money doesn't buy happiness, but at least you can suffer in comfort." Wise as she was, I've since learned that she didn't quite get it right; money *can* buy happiness, but only if you first save like mad, then spend those savings with care. Better than anyone I know, Jonathan understands and conveys this crucial bit of life calculus. Further, there's no one more qualified to do so: For more than a quarter century, he dispensed his unique brand of financial wisdom from his columns at *Forbes* and *The Wall Street Journal*—over a thousand in all—interspersed with five highly regarded books.

Most personal finance writers content themselves with the mechanics of saving, investing, insurance, credit, and the like. As his career progressed, Jonathan delved ever deeper: How does money make us happy or unhappy? What does it really represent to us? When should we spend, and on what? Why are we so bad at saving and investing?

On the surface, it all seems so obvious: We need money to buy the stuff that will make us happy. No, no, and no again. First and foremost, money buys time and autonomy. Secondarily, it buys experiences. Last, and least, it buys stuff, and more often than not, the stuff we buy makes us miserable.

Psychologists, in fact, tell us that we really don't know what makes us happy. We fantasize about retiring to a tropical paradise, but those who actually do soon find themselves hot, bored, and missing their friends and family. We lust after a Beemer and a 6,000 square foot house, only to find that they quickly lose their allure, and that maintaining them commands way too much time and money. Worst of all, the cost of all this stuff necessitates wasting our lives at jobs we despise and so prevents us from doing the things we love.

I don't want to play the spoiler, so I'll filter some of Jonathan's lesser points through my own experience:

1. We behave alarmingly like chickens. Our relentlessly materialistic culture addicts us to what

economists politely call "positional goods": the high-end car, handbag, or domicile that advertises our exalted place in the pecking order. You don't need to be a devotee of *Mad Men* to realize that what Madison Avenue *really* produces is discontent. The cure? A tolerant amusement, and perhaps even outright disdain, for those who think they are what they wear, drive, and dwell in.

2. Be careful, as already mentioned, of what you wish for. You just may get it and find that it isn't all it's cracked up to be, especially if it's a consumer durable item. The more durable it is, the longer it will remind you of what an unwise purchase it was. The things that are most likely to make you happy are time spent with friends and family, the pursuit of a lifelong passion, or enhancing your educational horizons. I used to dream of spending my summers in Copenhagen and winters in San Diego. The birth of my first grandchild taught me that if she lived in Cleveland, I just might move there.

3. We can't all retire at age 60. Given ever-increasing longevity, years of schooling and the alarming increase in the percentages of disabled adults, it's not too far-fetched to imagine a world in which the dependent, nonworking population exceeds the working one. This simply does not compute: Stocks and bonds are merely media of exchange among those who produce and those who consume, and as the number of workers producing the goods and services that retirees need falls, life for retirees who did not save prodigiously becomes ever more grim.

4. Everyone knows that stocks are risky, and academics like to make a parlor game out of just how bad that risk is. But there's a dimension to risk that gets relatively little attention: It's a function, more than anything else, of age. Because of what one hopes is a vigorous savings stream, stocks are really not that risky at all for the young saver. I'll go even further: A 20-something should get down on his knees and pray for a long, brutal bear market. In short, he should ardently embrace risk in order to acquire shares more cheaply. For the retiree, the situation is reversed: If she encounters a long bear market, spends more than 4 percent of her portfolio each year, and then encounters chronic medical problems, at best she's living with her kids, and at worst she's in a homeless shelter. In other words, for the retiree, stocks are Chernobyl risky.

5. Uncle Sam offers the best pension plan that money can buy: deferring Social Security until age 70. By spending down your retirement assets until then, you're in effect "buying" an annuity from him in the form of increased monthly payments. The payoff for this maneuver is an inflation-adjusted income stream of around 7.5 percent, far better than you can get from any insurance company, and which offers a free spousal survival benefit to boot. The takeaway: Don't even think about purchasing a commercial annuity product of any sort until you've spent down your nest egg to make it to 70.

6. Academics tout the idea of so-called consumption smoothing: borrowing heavily when you're young,

then paying off those debts when you're old, so as to maintain a constant standard of living throughout your life. This is a really, really dumb idea, since it ignores habituation: Get used to the Beemer and business class when you're young, and by the time you're middle-aged you'll need a Bentley and private jet. My medical colleague and fellow financial author Jim Dahle advises newly established doctors to continue "living like a resident" for several more years after starting practice. That's good advice for just about everyone else too: Get used to Motel 6 when you're young, and when you're older and richer you'll pinch yourself every time you check into the Sheraton.

7. The name of the game isn't to get rich; it's to not die poor. The quickest way to get filthy rich, of course, is to win the lottery, but if your investment strategy revolves around lottery tickets, you'll almost certainly die poor. The investment equivalent of the lottery ticket is looking for the next Apple or Starbucks, and your odds of succeeding are about the same as with a lottery ticket. In contrast, a portfolio of globally diversified stocks and bonds—and don't worry, Jonathan will show you just how easy this is to assemble and maintain these days—will never make you rich, but it does maximize your chance of a comfortable retirement.

8. Forget about trying to pick stocks; whenever you buy or sell, the person on the other side of the trade is likely Warren Buffett or Goldman Sachs. (And that's not even the worst-case scenario,

which is trading with an executive who knows more about his company than anyone else on the planet.) Again, to pick on my medical colleagues, many think that because they prescribe drugs, they have some special private knowledge about pharmaceutical companies; believe me, they don't. "Buying what you know" is a lousy strategy, and it applies to non-doctors as well.

9. The most important financial asset we bequeath to our kids is their unconscious adoption of our spending habits. If they've grown up watching you max out your mortgages and credit cards to buy stuff you don't need, you've likely poisoned their financial future.

With that appetizer out of the way, savor the fruit of Jonathan's decades at the forefront of personal finance journalism. Read, enjoy, profit, and, most critically, start yourself on the road to a richer life.

INTRODUCTION

T here are those who think the goal of investing is to beat the market and amass as much wealth as possible, that street smarts and hard work ensure investment success, and that the road to happiness is paved with more of everything.

And then there are those who get it.

I realize that sounds horribly arrogant. But in truth, those words are born of the humble realization that very few of us will beat the market, that saving diligently is the key to amassing wealth, that money buys limited happiness and that much of the time we are our own worst enemy.

This book is the product of 31 years of writing and thinking about money. For 25 of those years, I have been a financial journalist, my snotty nose pressed up against the window, trying to figure out what's happening on the inside. And for six years, as Director of Financial Education for Citigroup's U.S. wealth management business, I was on the inside, sneering at the people with their noses pressed up against the glass window.

Along the way, I did all the usual nonsense: bought actively managed mutual funds, dabbled in individual stocks, thought I knew what would happen next in the financial markets, and purchased stuff I was sure would make me endlessly happy. Again and again, I was proven wrong. There were no spectacular failures. But there were enough missteps that I was left with a nagging feeling that much of conventional wisdom wasn't especially wise.

In the pages ahead, what follows is how I have come to think about money, based on my own experience, a lifetime of reading, and thousands of conversations with ordinary investors, academics and finance professionals during my three decades kicking around Wall Street.

Money, alas, is befuddling to many folks. They imagine there's some great secret—a single investment product, a particular trading strategy, the musings of an investment guru—that will unlock vast wealth. But growing wealthy is actually embarrassingly simple: We save as much as we reasonably can, take on debt cautiously, limit our exposure to major financial risks and try not to be too clever with our investing. Early in our adult life, progress can be agonizingly slow, and it's easy to get discouraged. That first $100,000 can take many years to amass. If we stick to the simple, prudent path, however, the results can be astonishing. After a few decades, we might have $500,000—and that $500,000 can quickly become $1 million and maybe $2 million.

Problem is, while the path to wealth is simple, it isn't easy. In the next five chapters, I discuss five key steps that, I would argue, should be central to the way we handle money:

- There is a connection between money and happiness, but the relationship is far messier than most people imagine. If we want to get the most out of our dollars, we need to think much harder about how we spend and which goals we pursue.

- Most of us will live an amazingly long life that will often see us pursue more than one career and spend perhaps 20 or 30 years in retirement. That has big implications for how we handle our finances.

- Thanks to the instincts we inherited from our hunter-gatherer ancestors, we are hardwired to fail both as savers and as investors. Result: It takes great self-discipline—or, in the absence of self-discipline, a certain amount of self-deception—to manage money successfully.

- We divvy up our financial life into a series of buckets, thinking of our insurance policies as separate from our bank accounts, and our stock-bond investment mix as unrelated to our debts. But to manage money prudently and make the right tradeoffs, we need to bring together all these financial pieces—and the central organizing principle should be our paycheck, or lack thereof.

- To get ahead financially, we should think less about making our money grow and more about the dangers that could derail our financial future. This doesn't mean we shouldn't take risk by, say, investing heavily in the stock market or taking on a hefty mortgage to buy our first home. But even as we save and invest for the future, we should also aim to minimize potential subtractions from our wealth. Those subtractions might appear modest, like mutual fund expenses and stock trading costs, or they can be huge, such as selling shares at a market bottom or becoming disabled and yet not having disability insurance. Either way, there's the potential for great financial damage.

Among some readers, the ideas expressed in the pages that follow will prompt gnashing of teeth and grumblings of dissent. From the reactions I have received to my columns in *The Wall Street Journal* and elsewhere, I know various ideas—that money doesn't always buy happiness, that you're highly unlikely to beat the market, that paying ahead on a mortgage often makes sense, that retirees should delay claiming Social Security, that a retirement built around relaxing probably won't be satisfying—are profoundly unpopular. But I hope you will keep an open mind.

It isn't surprising that we find it tough to think clearly about money, given the obstacles in our way. In recent decades, there's been much focus on how ordinary folks handle money—and the research suggests we often shortchange ourselves. Academics who specialize in behavioral finance have found we don't behave rationally, as economists have traditionally assumed, but instead make numerous mental mistakes.

Similar insights have emerged from neuroeconomics, which looks at how the brain reacts in different financial scenarios. The prospect of a big win might trigger the release of dopamine and the accompanying feeling of euphoria, while an investment loss might lower the brain's serotonin level, leaving us anxious and irritable. Neuroeconomics provides confirmation for insights uncovered not only by behavioral finance but also by evolutionary psychology, which is the study of traits we inherited from our hunter-gatherer ancestors. Our Pleistocene brains were built to help us survive in the ancient world—but our instinctive reactions often hurt us when dealing with modern financial problems.

Meanwhile, other research has found that there isn't a simple relationship between money and happiness. Instead, all kinds of other factors appear to be important, including whether we are married, how far we commute and how old we are.[1]

While this book mentions a slew of different studies, it isn't intended to be a comprehensive survey. Instead, *How to Think About Money* is very much a personal view, where I draw on research findings that have resonated with me and have influenced how I look at the financial world. You will find footnotes for the key studies I have drawn on, but I haven't bothered to source every single fact or idea mentioned here.[2]

The insights from academia are often no surprise to financial advisors, particularly those who focus on so-called life planning, where the aim is to help folks use their money to lead a more fulfilling life, rather than merely to amass savings for standard goals like paying for college and retirement. Life planners frequently find that their clients don't know what they want to achieve with their financial life—and, in fact, may spend years making choices that are detrimental to their happiness.

Why do we get it wrong? There's no shortage of culprits. We are overly influenced by conventional wisdom and societal values. We pay too much heed to what our friends, family and especially our parents might think—even if our parents are no longer alive. We are driven by the instincts passed down from our nomadic ancestors. That hard wiring, which includes a great fear of losses and a constant desire to consume, isn't necessarily that helpful in today's world.

We are also heavily influenced by Wall Street and by corporate marketing. Financial firms want investors to believe that they can beat the market, because market-beating efforts are a great moneymaker—for Wall Street firms. Financial salespeople push whatever product compensates them. That means one salesperson might be plugging mutual funds and another might be flogging insurance. But it's rare that these salespeople will talk about how all these products fit into a customer's overall financial life, let alone discuss areas of financial planning where they don't have a product to sell, such as when to revise our wills, how to manage our 401(k) plan and when to claim Social Security. Meanwhile, the need to save for the future is often forgotten amid the endless stream of corporate advertising telling us it's time to buy a new car, a better laundry detergent or the latest frozen entrée. The message from the marketers is clear: The rich life consists of beautiful people who smile, laugh and never stop spending.

There is no conspiracy here. It's just the free market at work, with everybody pursuing his or her own self-interest. That everybody should include you. If we want a happy and successful financial life, where we squeeze the most out of our money, we need to cast aside wrongheaded conventional wisdom and ignore the self-serving prescriptions propagated by others—and instead figure out the right way to think about money.

BUY MORE HAPPINESS

To Get the Most Out of Our Money, We Need to Spend With Great Care

L ook around your living room. Check out the furniture, lamps and television. Glance at the pictures hanging on the walls. Wander into the kitchen. Let your eyes roam across the plates, bowls, cutlery and kitchen utensils. Take a peek in the bedroom, including all the clothes in your closet. Everywhere you look, there's stuff—stuff that you bought, often after careful consideration. You were confident that all these items would make your life happier. Have they? Or do you barely notice these items anymore—and, in some cases, perhaps even regret purchasing them?

Don't worry: I am not about to decry American

materialism or launch into some philosophical diatribe about the virtues of the monastic life. We all need chairs, cutlery and clothes. Instead, I want to emphasize a different point: We aren't very good at figuring out what will make us happy.

Classical economics assumes that individuals make choices that "maximize their utility," meaning that—while we may occasionally mess up—we don't regularly make choices that hurt our happiness. This is a dubious assumption. Many people smoke, overeat and watch hours of television every day, even though they wish they didn't.[3] Most folks spend too much today and save too little for the future. They choose careers that make them miserable. They buy homes that leave them with horribly long commutes. Our instinctive reactions may be helpful when assessing whether we are dealing with a friend or foe. But when deciding how to spend our time and money, and when settling on which goals to pursue, we shouldn't presume that we know instinctively what we want.

Still, there is hope. We can often figure out what we want upon reflection—and the academic research on money and happiness can help. A decade ago, I started reading the research and I was immediately hooked. This isn't touchy-feely nonsense spouted by pop psychology gurus, built on anecdotal evidence or driven by someone's philosophical or political views. Rather, the academic research is based on carefully controlled studies and rigorous analysis of large amounts of survey data.

The results have profound implications for how we handle our money and, more important, for how we lead our lives. Thanks to what I have learned from the research, I am quicker to make time for friends and family, even if it seems like an effort. I will happily spend money to visit my children or to bring them together for a family vacation or a special meal. I ditched my suburban New Jersey home so I could eliminate a long commute. I quit a high-paying job I had come to hate, because I knew I would be much happier if I spent my days engaged in activities that I thought were important and that I was passionate about.

Could the research change your life? Here are some of the surprising insights that have emerged from academic studies:

- Money can buy happiness, but not nearly as much as we imagine.

- We place too high a value on possessions and not enough on experiences.

- Spending money on others can deliver greater happiness than spending it on ourselves.[4]

- We're often happier when we have less choice, not more.

- Working hard toward our goals can bring great pleasure—but achieving our goals is often a letdown.

- Raising children isn't nearly as life-enhancing as many parents claim.

- Satisfaction through life appears to be U-shaped, with reported happiness falling through our 20s and 30s, hitting bottom in our 40s and bouncing back from there.

To be sure, other insights are less surprising: Those who are married, or who are surrounded by friends and family, tend to be happier. Ditto for the self-employed and those who exercise regularly. We also get a lot of pleasure from helping others. Meanwhile, commuting, ill health, unemployment and financial problems can bring unhappiness.

A 2006 Pew Research Center study found that Republicans were happier than Democrats and church goers were happier than those who stayed home on Sundays.[5] The study also found that those with and without pets and those with and without children were equally happy. As you might gather, there's a heap of research on what makes for a satisfying life, and many factors seem to be associated with differing degrees of life satisfaction.

Correlation, however, shouldn't be confused with causation. Maybe marriage or being in a long-term relationship makes people happier—that seems like a reasonable proposition—but it could be that happier people end up getting married. In addition, we're dealing here with averages. We can all think of married couples who are miserable and single individuals who are almost always happy. The challenge: We need to sort through the factors associated with varying degrees of life satisfaction and figure out which are most important, so we know what to focus on. Where to start? As we ponder the connection between money and happiness, I believe it's worth keeping four key ideas in mind.

First, happiness isn't a simple concept with a single definition. While a few good jokes and a couple of drinks can perk up a day, the focus here is less on momentary pleasure and more on what makes for a satisfying life. Moreover, whether we describe ourselves as happy depends on how the question is asked, as well as what happened in the minutes and hours that preceded the question. This is why the research sometimes reaches conflicting conclusions. An important distinction: Day-to-day happiness shouldn't be confused with the sense of contentment that we have—or don't have—when we sit back and contemplate our life.

Second, we often adapt quickly to both good and bad developments in our life. We are thrilled when we're told about the pay raise. A month later, the good feelings will likely have dissipated and the pay raise is just another paycheck. We fail to anticipate how quickly we will adapt, which is a key reason we are so bad at figuring out what will make us happy.

Third, happiness often depends on how we stand relative to others. Most of us would be thrilled to have $1 million in the bank. We would be less thrilled if we lived in a town where all our neighbors had $10 million.

Fourth, we all have different happiness "set points" that are genetically determined. Changing our life's circumstances and how we spend our days might raise or lower our happiness relative to this set point, but some folks will likely always be happier than others, no matter what life throws at them.

This set point might account for 50 percent of an individual's happiness level. Circumstances—our age, income, whether we're divorced—might determine another 10 percent. What about the remaining 40 percent? That's up to us. We can influence our level of happiness by how we choose to lead our life, including the goals we pursue, how we spend our money, and whether we volunteer, keep our commute short and make an effort to see friends and family.[6]

RUNNING THE TREADMILL

Of all the puzzles surrounding happiness, the connection with money is perhaps the most perplexing. We might read about a celebrity who is both wealthy and miserable, and glibly declare, "Money, of course, doesn't buy happiness." Yet we can't help thinking that we would indeed be happier if we were richer.

So does money buy happiness? In poorer parts of the world, the question would strike folks as absurd. If we lift people out of poverty, so they no longer worry about basic needs like food and shelter, we can vastly improve their happiness. In low-income countries such as Kenya, Tanzania and Uganda, people express much less satisfaction with their lives than in middle-income countries like China, Peru and South Africa.[7] But what happens after that? Does more money buy ever more happiness? It seems not: Life satisfaction in advanced countries like Germany, the U.K. and the U.S. isn't notably higher than in middle-income countries.

Economist Richard Easterlin was the first to highlight the shaky connection between money and happiness. In 1974, he pointed out what's now known as the Easterlin paradox: Even though the U.S. and other developed countries had grown wealthier over the decades, their reported level of happiness hadn't climbed. More money, it seems, hadn't brought—or bought—greater happiness.

"Taken all together, how would you say things are these days? Would you say that you are very happy, pretty happy or not too happy?" Since 1972, this question has been asked every year or two as part of the General Social Survey. The survey is conducted by NORC, which is headquartered on the University of Chicago's campus (and which used to be known as the National Opinion Research Center).

In 2014, 32.5 percent of Americans said they were very happy, versus a 42-year average of 33.3 percent. The survey also found that 27 percent were satisfied with their financial situation, compared with a 42-year average of 29.6 percent. Over the intervening four decades, U.S. inflation-adjusted disposable income per capita grew 108 percent. The great conundrum: We have twice as much to spend as we had 42 years ago—but our reported level of happiness is no higher and our satisfaction with our financial situation has declined.

Why hasn't more money brought greater happiness? I remember writing a column about the weak link between money and happiness. One reader, who obviously disagreed, noted that money can buy a jet ski—and you never see an unhappy person on a jet ski. That may be true. But what if you rode the jet ski every day? How long would the thrill last?

At issue here is the so-called hedonic treadmill or hedonic adaptation. The notion: We aspire to get that next promotion and, initially, we are thrilled when the promotion comes through. But all too quickly, we adapt to our improved circumstances, we take the new job for granted and soon we're hankering after something else. We can probably blame this cycle of striving, adaptation and disenchantment on our hunter-gatherer ancestors. We are here today because they were never satisfied with what they had and instead, in their quest for survival, strove relentlessly for more.

Adaptation may also explain why we are often happier if we have less choice. The freedom to choose is much valued in American society, but it also breeds uncertainty—and uncertainty can be the death of happiness. If we don't like where we live but we can't afford to move, we adapt. But if we have enough money to move tomorrow, we might never adapt and instead wrestle with the decision every day, trying to figure out whether we should stay put or buy a home somewhere else. Happiness lies not in the choice, but in making a decision and eliminating the choice.

The process of striving for material improvements, and then quickly adapting to those improvements, makes it difficult to achieve permanent increases in our level of happiness. But adaptation also has a silver lining: It can help save us from everlasting misery. We imagine that we will never recover from divorce, a family member's death or a permanently disabling injury. And yet we do. Adaptation helps explain why our life's circumstances account for a relatively modest 10 percent of our overall happiness.[8]

While we adapt to changes in our circumstances, the degree of adaptation varies. We quickly get used to the new car, and soon our level of happiness is back where it started. What if we have chronic health problems or our spouse leaves us? We might swiftly recover from our initial distress—but we might never be as happy as when we were healthy and married.

The link between money and happiness is clearly more complicated than we imagine. But that doesn't mean there's no connection. To get a handle on the issue, it is helpful to distinguish between how folks evaluate their life and how they assess their day-to-day emotional well-being.

In the U.S., it seems day-to-day happiness rises along with income until you hit roughly $75,000 a year. After that, income doesn't appear to matter. Moreover, money is hardly the dominant factor in determining day-to-day happiness. Other factors, like ill health, loneliness and caring for another adult, are also crucial. In addition, smoking is associated with lower levels of emotional well-being.[9]

But surely a higher income would make day-to-day life more pleasant? It seems not. For one study, 374 workers were asked about the intensity of various feelings at 25-minute intervals throughout the day. Those with higher incomes reported being no happier, but they were more likely to say they had feelings of anger and hostility or they felt anxious or tense.[10] On top of this added stress, higher-paying jobs can involve longer hours, leaving us with less time for other activities, notably socializing with friends and family, which can deliver a big boost to happiness.

What if we look beyond day-to-day happiness and consider someone's evaluation of his or her life? There, money appears to play a more important role, with reported levels of happiness rising fairly steadily with income. The implication: Even if a higher income doesn't necessarily improve how much people enjoy the day to day, it does make them view their life more favorably.[11]

This might seem like the green light to pursue the material life and gun for the highest income possible. But before you start working weekends so you win that next pay raise, give some thought to so-called focusing illusions. "Does Living in California Make People Happy?" For a study with that title, almost 2,000 undergraduates were surveyed at four colleges, two in the Midwest and two in California.

Students in the two regions reported no difference in their overall satisfaction with their lives—and yet they both expected someone living in California to be more satisfied than someone living in the Midwest. What's going on here? When students imagined living in the Midwest and living in California, they focused on easily observed differences between the two regions, notably the better California weather. Their mistake: They failed to appreciate that happiness with the weather isn't that important to satisfaction with one's overall life.[12]

Could the same be true of money and happiness? In other words, when we are asked whether we are satisfied with our life, does our attention immediately turn to how much we earn and how much money we have amassed—and that prompts those with more to say they're happier?

Even if the link between money and happiness is a focusing illusion, you could use this illusion to your benefit. Suppose that last year you had the kitchen remodeled, but now you barely notice your expensive renovation. You may be able to squeeze a little more happiness out of the money spent by pausing for a moment, contemplating your stainless steel Sub-Zero refrigerator and thinking how lucky you are.

CONSUMING UNHAPPINESS

The research suggests money can improve day-to-day happiness, at least up to a point, and also make us feel better when we sit back and reflect on our life. But the pursuit of money—and how we spend it—can also hurt our happiness. In particular, we make three major mistakes.

The first mistake: We put ourselves in a position where we feel relatively deprived. This again is a focusing illusion, but one that works to our disadvantage. Let's say we get a big pay raise and that prompts us to buy a home in a more desirable neighborhood. A good idea? Maybe not. It seems that, if our neighbors earn more than we do, we are likely to be unhappy, especially if we regularly spend time with them.[13]

The impact of our neighbors—and how our position compares to theirs—also affects those in financial difficulty. A study looked at families in the U.K. that were struggling with debt. Those living in areas where such problems were common were less unhappy than those living in more prosperous areas.[14] Misery, it seems, really does love company.

If moving into a town with wealthier neighbors can hurt our happiness, it can be doubly bad if that neighborhood is farther from work. This is the second major mistake that folks make. Research suggests commuting is terrible for happiness. A study of 909 employed women in Texas looked at their assessment of 19 activities they undertook during the day. The worst-ranked activity was the morning commute and the third-worst was the evening commute.[15]

Commuting doesn't just reduce happiness. It can also wreck relationships. A study in Sweden found that a commute of at least 45 minutes increased the risk that a couple would separate by as much as 40 percent. The risk was lower if one or both spouses or partners had been commuting for more than five years or if they had been long-distance commuters before the relationship began.[16]

Okay, so we don't want a long commute or

wealthier neighbors. Anything else? Let's continue with the real estate theme: Suppose we are thinking of buying a much bigger house. As we contemplate the new home, we might be captivated by all the extra space we will have, as well as the big yard for the kids to play in.

We probably won't give much thought to the greater upkeep involved. Even if we don't do the work ourselves, and instead hire others to mow the lawn, clean the house and do occasional repairs, we will still have the hassle of finding others to do these chores.

That brings us to the third major mistake: We are inclined to use our money to buy more and more possessions, because we value possessions for their ongoing value. But in fact we are often happier when we spend our money on experiences rather than things. Why? There are numerous possible reasons.[17]

Experiences not only offer the chance for eager anticipation, but they can also leave us with fond memories—and those memories often grow fonder over time, as we recall the overall event and forget the incidental annoyances. Meanwhile, we quickly adapt to material improvements in our life, plus we have to care for these possessions and watch them deteriorate.

Experiences also become part of our identity in a way that material goods don't. We might even have mixed feelings about the stuff we acquire, because we fear we will be viewed as materialistic. By contrast, experiences can increase our sense of community. We often share them with other people and afterwards we can laugh about them with our companions. We can also regale other friends, who weren't there, with stories of our adventures.

Remember how wealthy neighbors can make us feel

relatively deprived and hence less happy? Similarly, there will always be somebody with more and better possessions. But they won't necessarily have better experiences. The fact is, it's hard to compare the quality of our experiences to those enjoyed by others. Want to get more happiness out of your dollars? Forget the flat-screen television—and instead go for the memorable vacation.

RAISING HELL

Now we come to a touchy topic: Do children help or hurt happiness? This is the point at which I hastily mention that I have two children and two stepchildren, so I can't be accused of being a self-absorbed, childless New Yorker. Instead, I have clearly cast my vote in favor of reproduction. Yet the evidence on this one is mixed.

A November 2012 Pew Research Center survey found that, among married adults, 36 percent of those with children and 39 percent of those without children described themselves as "very happy." What about folks who are single? Among those with children, 23 percent said they were very happy. Among those who didn't have children, the "very happy" group was even smaller, at 22 percent.[18]

This tells us that married couples tend to be happier than those who are single. But what happens when we add children to the mix? As the Pew Research data suggests, it isn't clear children help happiness, and it doesn't get much clearer when we look at academic studies. There are well-researched articles that argue that children hurt happiness—and other research that argues just the opposite.

One intriguing study suggests that the gap between

the happiness of parents and non-parents has narrowed over time. The authors' contention: Social fragmentation and economic insecurity have driven down the happiness of those without kids. Parents are less affected by these trends, in part because having children helps parents to socialize more.[19]

Where does this leave us? It appears children are a mixed blessing—at least when it comes to happiness. As Angus Deaton and Arthur Stone write, "We find little difference in subjective wellbeing between people with and without children." They note that "people who live with children are more likely to be married, richer, better educated, more religious, and healthier"—all factors associated with greater reported happiness.[20]

What if we control for these factors, so we isolate the impact of having children? Deaton and Stone found that raising kids is a mixed bag in terms of day-to-day happiness, with parents suffering more stress but also enjoying more fun moments. Overall, U.S. parents evaluate their life slightly less favorably. I find this a little surprising: I would have thought that parents would have judged their lives to be richer than those who had no kids. I feel like raising children has given a meaning and purpose to my life that would have been missing if I had had neither children nor stepchildren. But the research suggests that perhaps I am wrong.

SPENDING RIGHT

Wealthy neighbors, long commutes and acquiring possessions can hurt happiness, and children don't appear to help much. But this doesn't mean money can't buy happiness. Academics Elizabeth Dunn,

Daniel Gilbert and Timothy Wilson don't waste any time, packing their argument into the title of their 2011 article: "If money doesn't make you happy, then you probably aren't spending it right."[21]

As the authors note, "Money allows people to live longer and healthier lives, to buffer themselves against worry and harm, to have leisure time to spend with friends and family, and to control the nature of their daily activities—all of which are sources of happiness. Wealthy people don't just have better toys; they have better nutrition and better medical care, more free time and more meaningful labor—more of just about every ingredient in the recipe for a happy life. And yet, they aren't that much happier than those who have less. If money can buy happiness, then why doesn't it? Because people don't spend it right."

So how can we buy ourselves happiness? The authors mention a number of strategies—many of them counterintuitive. We get greater happiness if we spend our money on others rather than on ourselves. We will likely get more pleasure from frequent small purchases than occasional big expenditures. We also get more pleasure if we delay purchases rather than buying items right away, because the delay brings with it an enjoyable stretch of anticipation.

The authors suggest that, when assessing the impact of a purchase or event on our life, we shouldn't focus so much on the big picture. Forget thoughts such as, "Wouldn't it be great to own a vacation home?" Instead, we should think more about the mundane details, like what a hassle it would be to deal with maintenance and repairs. Such headaches are a big influence on day-to-day happiness. In addition, the authors note that comparison shopping can lead us to focus on features that aren't that important. For instance, when house-hunting, we might be drawn to bigger, more expensive homes. But there's a good chance our home's size won't prove all that important to our long-run happiness, and yet we could find ourselves spending far more than we should.

By this point in the chapter, many readers will likely be in a word fog. You have heard about all these factors associated with higher and lower levels of happiness. You have also heard about ways that money can help your happiness—and ways it can hurt. So what should you do? In my own life, I endeavor to focus on three broad themes.

Psychology professors Edward Deci and Richard Ryan are the fathers of so-called self-determination theory. They have posited that we have three basic psychological needs: the need for competence, relatedness and autonomy. These needs—when satisfied—lead to greater self-motivation and the experience of well-being.[22]

To this, you might respond, "What the heck are they talking about?" Basically, we're happier and more enthused about our daily life if we are engaged in activities we feel we are good at (competence), we are doing them because we want to rather than because we're being forced to (autonomy) and we aren't socially isolated (relatedness). Along the same lines, I believe that, if we are smart in how we handle our finances, we can use money to boost our happiness in three ways.

First, money can ease our financial worries and help us to achieve a greater sense of autonomy. As I see it, money is sort of like health. It is only when we're sick that we realize how wonderful it is to feel healthy. Similarly, it's only when we don't have enough money that we realize how great it is to be on a solid financial footing. More money may not make us happy—but not having money could make us extremely unhappy. We might feel boxed in by our financial obligations or feel like we can't change careers, even though we have come to hate our current job.

Yes, we ought to save for retirement, a house down payment and the kids' college education. But these specific goals fall within a broader, overriding financial objective: We want to get ourselves to the point where money isn't something that we regularly fret about or that tightly constrains how we lead our lives. There are plenty of fine books and articles devoted to the nitty-gritty of paying down debt, building up savings, investing prudently, managing taxes, planning an estate and so on.[23] But the ultimate objective is always the same: We want to seize control of our finances, so we have more control over our lives. As our debts shrink and our savings grow, we come to enjoy an ever greater degree of financial freedom. This culminates with retirement, at which point our time is our own, with no need to earn a paycheck.

Second, money can allow us to spend our days doing what we love and what we feel we're good at. This is the sense of competence that Deci and Ryan say we need. Meeting this need shouldn't be a distant fantasy, reserved for when we finally have enough money to retire, but rather something we should strive for during our working years. We will discuss this further in the next chapter, where we delve into the intriguing notion of "flow" and tackle the difference between "extrinsic" and "intrinsic" motivation.

Third, money can make it possible to have special times with those we care about. Research suggests that a robust network of friends and family can be a huge source of happiness. Even dealing with people in passing—the cashier at the supermarket, the parking lot attendant, the barista at Starbucks—can increase our sense of belonging to a community.

We may embrace the American ideal of rugged individualism. But most of us are also social creatures who want to connect with others and who care deeply about our reputation. Think about it: Why are we polite to strangers we will never see again? Why do we leave a tip at restaurants we will never go back to?

One implication: We should think twice before moving to another part of the country, especially upon retirement. Like the Midwest students who assumed people in California were happier, we shouldn't assume that the warmer weather in Arizona or Florida will somehow compensate for the friends we leave behind in Michigan.

Earlier, we discussed the study of 909 employed women in Texas and how they assessed 19 daily activities.[24] Commuting ranked at the bottom in terms of daily happiness. Work also didn't rate well. What activities did bring happiness? Just 11 percent of the women mentioned engaging in what the researchers delicately referred to as "intimate relations." On average, these intimate relations lasted just 13 minutes. But they topped the charts in terms of happiness.

The second-highest-ranked item was more significant—at least in terms of its broad impact on happiness. The women gave "socializing after work" high marks, and it took up an average 69 minutes of the day. Make no mistake: Spending time with friends and family is a key contributor to happiness. But we don't need an academic study to tell us that. Not many of us would choose to eat alone in a restaurant when we could be eating with others. Ditto for watching a movie, shopping, cleaning up the yard and a host of other activities.

Friends and family aren't just good for happiness. They are also good for our health. A 2010 study pulled together data from 148 earlier studies that contained information on the connection between mortality and the frequency of interaction with others.[25] The authors found that the boost to longevity from a strong network of friends and family was roughly equal to the boost we get by quitting smoking. (What if we insist on smoking? Based on the studies, it seems we should never, ever smoke alone.)

Earlier, I mentioned that we get greater happiness from experiences, rather than possessions. To squeeze additional happiness out of those experiences, be sure to include friends and family. When you go for a hike, go with somebody else. Get concert tickets for you and a colleague. Take the kids on a cruise. Arrange a family reunion. Go out to dinner with friends. Fly across the country to see the grandchildren.

To be sure, a family meal out or attending a concert might last just a few hours, and yet it can cost far more than, say, a Kindle Fire HD notebook computer that lets you answer emails, read e-books, watch movies, listen to music and surf the web. Possessions are often a bargain, while experiences tend to be expensive. Moreover, paying for all those restaurant meals and family vacations will leave less wealth to bequeath to our children.

Still, creating great family memories strikes me as one of the best ways to spend money. There have been 43 U.S. presidents.[26] No doubt all of them thought they had achieved some measure of immortality. Yet today, you would be hard pressed to find anyone who can name all 43 presidents, let alone tell you much about each. If immortality is proving elusive for U.S. presidents, there isn't much hope for the rest of us. Five or 10 years after we are gone, most of us will be forgotten—except by family and close friends. We will live on in their memories. That's the closest any of us will ever get to immortality, at least on this earth. My advice: Make sure the memories are good.

BET ON A LONG LIFE

Most of Us Will Enjoy Extraordinarily Long Lives—And That Has Profound Financial Implications

R oughly 10,000 years ago, humans settled down and started rudimentary farms, on which they grew crops and kept animals. What kept us busy during the 1.8 million years prior to that? We were nomads who fished, hunted and foraged for edible wild plants. There was no thought about which animals to domesticate and feed, or what crops to cultivate during the next growing season. Instead, for almost all of human history, long-term planning consisted of figuring out what was for dinner.

We have evolved somewhat in the 10,000 years since our ancestors started putting down roots, but our ability to look ahead doesn't appear to be much improved. Most of us have a good handle on today and a fair idea of what needs to get done in the week ahead. We have half an eye on the big work deadline that's three weeks away and we have spent a little time on the Internet, gathering ideas for next summer's vacation. But what about planning for the next few years—or for the next few decades? Much of the time, we are just muddling through, fixated on making it through the day and barely aware of the wonderfully long life ahead of us.

How long? If you were a man born in the U.S. in 1900, your life expectancy at birth was age 52. If you were a woman, it was age 58. By 2000, life expectancy at birth had climbed roughly 50 percent, to age 80 for men and age 84 for women. Impressed? For those hoping to live to a ripe old age, there's good news and bad news.

The bad news: While male life expectancy climbed 28 years during the 20th century and female life expectancy rose 26 years, a large part of the increase was due to falling infant mortality, rather than rising life expectancies for those who made it to adulthood. Moreover, the bulk of the improvement in life expectancy—20 years in the case of both men and women—occurred during the first half of the 20th century. The pace of improvement has slowed significantly since then, and it's expected to continue slowing. The Social Security Administration projects that, for men born in 2100, life expectancy will be just seven years longer than it was in 2000, while women's life expectancy will be just six years longer.[27] Medical advances could change that, of course. But it seems the biggest improvements in life expectancy are behind us.

Maybe all of our great-great-grandchildren won't be regularly living to 100.

There is, however, also good news: The longer we live, the longer we can expect to live. When today's 65-year-olds were born in 1951, the life expectancy was age 73 for men and age 79 for women. But those figures include all the unlucky individuals who never made it to age 65. Among those born in 1951 who are still alive today, the life expectancy is age 84 for men and 87 for women. Keep in mind that these are medians, which means half of all folks will live to these ages or longer. Among today's 65-year-olds, roughly 25 percent will live to at least age 90 and 10 percent to at least age 95.

If you count yourself among America's upper middle class, there's an especially good chance that you will live to celebrate your 90th birthday. Consider the life expectancies used by insurance companies when they price income annuities. Insurers base their prices not on the general population, but on the healthy, affluent individuals who tend to be their customers. Insurers assume that a man who is currently age 65 will live to age 88, on average, while a woman will live to age 90.[28] That's three or four years longer than the life expectancy for the broad population. A long life is starting to look like a luxury good, with wealthier Americans enjoying lengthy retirements, while those with less money often suffer an earlier demise.

All this should change the way we think about money. Today, we are engaged in a vast, real-life, real-time experiment, where we have millions of people not only spending unprecedented amounts of time in the workforce, but also unprecedented amounts of time in retirement. We need to figure out what will keep us happily employed for four decades and perhaps longer. We need to figure out how to pay for a retirement of uncertain length, but which could easily last 20 or 30 years. And we need to figure out what we'll do with all that free time.

If you buy into conventional wisdom, there's no need to do any figuring out. According to the traditional conception of a successful life, we should bust our chops for 40 years, saving as much as we can, paying into Social Security and perhaps becoming vested in a traditional employer pension plan. For our efforts, we're rewarded in our 60s: We get to retire, kick back and spend our remaining days blissfully doing nothing. Sound like a prescription for happiness? It's more like a recipe for misery. We might commit four decades to working at a job we hate and then devote two or three decades to relaxing, which is hardly the most fulfilling way to spend our time.

Moreover, even if this sort of life sounds desirable, it almost certainly isn't sustainable. In 2005, we had 4.8 adults age 20 to 64 for every person age 65 or older. Today, the ratio is 3.9 to 1 and, by 2030, it'll be down to 2.7 to 1.[29] You and I may be able to save like crazy, so we can still retire at age 65. But as the population of senior citizens grows ever larger, not everybody can quit the workforce at 65.[30] Those still working simply couldn't produce enough goods and services to meet the needs of the entire population. One way or another, we need the retirement age to climb. That might be driven by lower investment returns, rising inflation or cuts in Social Security, or some combination of these and other factors that put financial pressure on older Americans and prod them to stay in the workforce for longer.[31]

What does all this mean for how we handle our money? I would argue that today's impressive life expectancy has four key financial implications. First, we need to get ourselves on the right financial track as early in our adult life as possible, so we quickly achieve some measure of financial freedom. Second, we should use that freedom to focus on work we're passionate about. Third, we should invest for the long-term, and that means making a lifetime commitment to stocks. Finally, when managing money, we should worry less about dying young and more about living an astonishingly long life. In the pages ahead, we'll tackle each of these four notions.

BUYING FREEDOM

When I talk to college students, I don't tell them to follow their dreams. Instead, I tell them to focus on making and saving money. I even suggest that they might deliberately opt for a less interesting but higher-paying job, so they can sock away serious sums of money.

All this might sound deadly dull and horribly reactionary. Aren't those in their 20s meant to pursue their passions, before they become burdened by the demands of raising a family and making the monthly mortgage payment? Underpinning this is an implicit—but rarely examined—assumption: that pursuing our passions is somehow more important in our 20s than in our 50s. I think this is nonsense. In fact, I think just the opposite is true.

Bear with me while I try to clamber out of the hole I just dug for myself.

As we learned in chapter 1, many purchases don't bring much happiness, so those who adopt a frugal lifestyle in their 20s and 30s probably won't be missing out on much. Those fast cars, big houses and electronic toys may be alluring, but they will likely bring only the briefest of pleasure. Meanwhile, it is mighty tough to amass enough money for a retirement that could last 30 years. If we start young, we will find it far easier. We will have more years to save money and we'll enjoy many decades of investment compounding.

Perhaps most important, we might spend 40 years or more in the workforce, and we need to be prepared for upheaval. Even if we aren't forced to change careers by global competition or disruptive new technologies, there's a good chance we will want to change. Four decades is an awfully long time to do the same thing. When we enter the workforce in our 20s, we might be thrilled with our chosen career. By our 40s, the thrill will likely be gone, we might be deeply unhappy with our job, and our greatest daily ambition may be to head home and hit the scotch bottle. Want to avoid that fate? If we get ourselves in great financial shape early in our adult life, we could spend our remaining decades with far fewer money worries—and with the financial freedom to change careers, perhaps to a job that's less lucrative but which we might find more fulfilling.

Economists engaged in happiness research have found that our satisfaction through life is U-shaped.[32] It appears that our happiness declines through our 20s and 30s, hits bottom in our 40s and then rebounds from there. Later life can be among our happiest times, until our happiness is dragged down by health issues.

What explains the U-shape, which seems to provide graphical proof that the midlife crisis is a real phenomenon? It might be simply that middle age is a time when we are under the most stress. We're struggling to raise kids, while also forging ahead with our career and perhaps even helping our elderly parents.

Alternatively, it could be that our waning happiness through our early adult years reflects a growing realization that we won't achieve all of our youthful ambitions and that we will leave only the smallest of marks on the world. Eventually, we come to terms with this, and that is when our happiness rebounds.

This latter explanation strikes me as convincing. When we are younger, seeking accolades can be all consuming. We desperately want the pay raises and promotions. A few years ago, a boss I had described the corporate world as "unnatural," and he said it wasn't surprising that people were unhappy and treated colleagues in ways they would never treat friends. But when we are younger, the work world doesn't seem unnatural. Rather, it is novel and fascinating. We are anxious to figure out the rules, find our place and prove our worth. To those in their 20s and 30s, working at a relatively uninspiring job may not seem like such a burden—and it could be a smart financial move if it comes with a fat paycheck that allows us to sock away a healthy sum every month.

But after a decade or two in the workforce, our orientation often shifts. We know the office rules. We have had some success, even if it wasn't as much as we had hoped. We have discovered that the promotions and pay raises—and the material goods they allow us to buy—provide only fleeting happiness. We have grown increasingly cynical about the workplace, with its office politics and frequent layoffs. Meanwhile, with any luck, we have started to amass some savings. As our sense of financial security grows, earning money becomes less of a motivator. Most crucially, we come to know ourselves better and we learn what we find most fulfilling.

Academic psychologists distinguish between external (or extrinsic) and internal (or intrinsic) motivation. External motivation can be either a carrot, like the possibility of a pay raise, or a stick, such as the fear of getting fired. By contrast, intrinsic motivation comes from within. Conceivably, intrinsic motivation could be negative, such as the fear we will feel badly if we eat the entire box of Oreos. But typically, it's viewed as something highly positive: We aren't acting because somebody is cajoling us with carrots and sticks, but because of a burning desire within. As the self-employed and small business owners can attest, work rarely feels like a chore when it's your choice, rather than somebody else's command.

Intrinsic motivation is lauded in a variety of celebrated psychological theories. Edward Deci and Richard Ryan's self-determination theory, mentioned at the end of chapter 1, discusses three core psychological needs: relatedness, competence and autonomy. When these needs are satisfied, we enjoy a greater sense of well-being and we are more likely to be self-motivated. At the top of Abraham Maslow's famous hierarchy of needs sits "self-actualization," where we are driven not by external forces, but by a desire to fully realize our inner potential. Intrinsic motivation is also central to Mihaly Csikszentmihalyi's notion of "flow," the state of total absorption in an activity. We'll talk more about flow later in this chapter.

As we reach our 40s, external carrots and sticks may no longer loom so large. Instead, we are more drawn to activities we find personally fulfilling. The result can be a growing sense of disenchantment with the workplace and with our life, and we may find ourselves bumping along the bottom of the U-shaped curve. That might sound grim, but arguably it's a crucial transition on the way to becoming a fully mature, self-aware adult. To regain our happiness, we must cast aside our single-minded drive to collect external rewards, and instead pursue goals that matter most to us, rather than to others.

Seem reasonable? Unfortunately, the research is inconclusive.[33] As we age, some of us become less motivated by external rewards and more focused on what we find intrinsically satisfying. But it isn't clear that this happens to most people. A big reason, I suspect, is money. Many people reach the point where they have the financial leeway to pursue the goals they find intrinsically satisfying. But others never get there. Maybe they put off saving money until later in life—or maybe they weren't able to save. Perhaps they had stretches when they couldn't find work. Perhaps they suffered from ill health and had to grapple with the related medical bills. Perhaps they simply never earned much money. Whatever the reason, external rewards remain important for many people in their 50s and 60s because, alas, they have no other choice.

All this can make talk of "self-actualization" and "intrinsic motivation" sound like fanciful nonsense only attainable by the financially comfortable. There's some truth to that. But these notions are also built on an undeniable contention: Given a choice, wouldn't you rather spend your time doing what you are passionate about, rather than devoting your days to work that others deem important?

For some, this choice will seem false. They love their work, so they get to pursue their passions, while also getting paid. But many others aren't so lucky. They reach their 40s and the career that carried them through their first two decades in the workforce no longer seems so thrilling. They cast around for what to do next—and often settle on a career they think will be more fulfilling, but perhaps doesn't pay as much. Think about the investment banker who becomes a high school math teacher, the corporate executive who quits to join a nonprofit organization, or the middle manager who launches his or her own business. In many cases, these folks give up safe jobs and hefty amounts of dollar income in order to enjoy more psychic income.

It turns out that this more fulfilling work can also be good for our health. Lauren Schmitz, a research fellow at the University of Michigan, looked at the connection between working conditions and health for workers age 50 and older. "Occupations that allow men to use their strongest abilities and give them a sense of achievement, independence, variety, authority, creativity, and status are associated with improved health at older ages," Schmitz writes. She says the impact was equal in magnitude to the effect of exercising vigorously three times a week or more.[34]

Considering a midlife career change? Many workers try it, and most are successful. For a 2015 study, the American Institute for Economic Research looked at career changes after age 45. Roughly half the respondents had changed careers for economic reasons and half for reasons that weren't strictly financial. Among the 82 percent of respondents who successfully changed careers, many took on work that used many of the skills they already had. Half saw their income rise, 18 percent said their income stayed the same and 31 percent saw their income fall. Changing careers seems to have helped happiness: 65 percent said they felt less stress at work and 87 percent said they were happy or very happy with the change.[35]

Making a midlife career change, with all the risk it entails, will be far easier if we have saved diligently since we entered the workforce. The more money we have, the more options we have. That doesn't mean change won't be stressful. It's nerve-racking to give up a secure job, even one we have come to dislike, and wrestling with that decision may prove to be a source of temporary unhappiness. Yet it is undoubtedly better than the alternative: If we haven't amassed much in savings, we may have no choice but to get up tomorrow and go back to a job we have come to loathe.

GOING WITH THE FLOW

If financial freedom is the ability to spend our days doing what we want, rather than being beholden to others, what is it that we should do? "Taking it easy" and "having fun" might come to mind. And certainly, as discussed in the last chapter, there's great happiness to be found in experiences and in spending time with friends and family. But I would also focus on doing work that we truly enjoy.

There is a reason the world's gardens are full of benches that nobody ever sits on. As distant relatives of our hunter-gatherer ancestors, we aren't built for leisure or built to relax. Rather, we are built to strive. We are often happiest when we are engaged in activities that we think are important, we are passionate about, we find challenging and we think we are good at. This is captured by the notion of "flow," a concept developed by Claremont Graduate University psychology professor Mihaly Csikszentmihalyi (whose name, apparently, is pronounced "me high – chick sent me high").[36]

You can think of a surgeon in the operating room, a painter or writer lost in his or her work, or a sports professional intensely focused on the game at hand. Even everyday activities—cooking dinner, driving to work, doing the taxes—offer the chance for flow, though we are more likely to have these moments if it's a task we are actively engaged in, rather than passive activities such as watching television. When we are in the midst of highly challenging activities to which we bring a high level of skill, we can become totally absorbed in what we are doing and lose all sense of time.

These moments of flow might not be happy in the conventional sense—we aren't laughing out loud with our buddies—and yet they can be among our most satisfying times. We enjoy the activity for its own sake and the ultimate goal is relatively unimportant. We love the feeling that we're making progress. The journey— striving toward our goals—often brings greater satisfaction than reaching the destination. Once again, we are back on the hedonic treadmill: As soon as we achieve a goal, the brief sense of exhilaration quickly gives way to dissatisfaction.

Thanks to increasing life expectancies, many of us will have long careers and long retirements. We will likely need more than one passion to carry us through our 40-plus years in the workforce and our 20 or 30 years in retirement. Think of the story of the dog that spends every day chasing cars down the street. Finally, after years of chasing, he catches a car, wrapping his great, slobbering jaw around the back bumper. That's when the question pops into the dog's head: "So what the heck do I do now?"

For some, this thought will slowly dawn on them in their 40s or 50s, as they come to realize that, even if they still care about the work world's external rewards, they no longer need them. For others, this thought will strike suddenly, when they quit the workforce. We toil for 40-plus hours a week for 48 weeks a year for 40 years, all so we can snag that great, tantalizing prize known as retirement. Then what? Retirement has the potential to be the happiest, most fulfilling time in our life. But it isn't guaranteed. A major mistake: Many folks spend decades preparing financially for retirement, but they give scant thought to what they will do with all that free time. We likely won't be happy spending day after day getting up slowly, reading the newspaper and playing golf. That might make us happy for a week or two. But soon enough, we will grow restless. As many retirees discover, endless leisure can quickly become endless boredom.

Even in retirement, we need a reason to get out of bed in the morning—something that will give a sense of purpose to our days—and, if it also makes us a little money, all the better. Realistically, in a world of more than 7 billion people, nothing any of us do is that significant. Still, we hunger for the feeling that we're doing something important with our time. My contention: The conventional distinction between work and retirement—between being productive and suddenly being unproductive—doesn't serve retirees well. Instead, retirement should be viewed as a continuation of our time in the workforce: We still need fulfilling work. The only difference, in retirement, is that we don't have to worry so much about whether that work comes with a paycheck.

Are you looking ahead to retirement and contemplating how to use your remaining decades? Are you in midlife and burned out on your current career? Some readers will already know what they want to do. For others, it will take considerable thought. What work will you find personally satisfying? What will give you those moments of flow? In search of an answer, try asking yourself these questions:

- Imagine money were not an issue. What would you do with your time?

- Suppose you were writing your obituary. What accomplishments would you like to be remembered for?

- Look back through your life. When were you happiest—and what were you doing?

- Think about your current job. Which parts of the job do you enjoy the most?

- Consider the careers you didn't pursue, perhaps because they didn't pay enough or because the chances of success seemed too uncertain. Now that you don't need a paycheck or can live on a smaller income, should you entertain those career possibilities again?

You might also ask yourself the three questions developed by George Kinder, author of *The Seven Stages of Money Maturity* and founder of the Kinder Institute of Life Planning, which trains financial advisors. Kinder's questions are designed to help folks figure out what they want to do with their lives.

- Imagine you have enough saved to satisfy all your financial needs for the rest of your life. Would you change your life and, if so, how would you change it?

- Assume you are in your current financial situation. Your doctor tells you that you only have five to 10 years to live, but that you will feel fine up until the end. Would you change your life and, if so, how would you change it?

- Your doctor tells you that you have a single day left to live. You look back over your life. What did you miss out on? Who did you not get to be? What did you fail to do?[37]

As you zero in on things you would like to do with your retirement or with your remaining time in the workforce, try to test drive your dreams. You might be captivated by the idea of becoming a docent at an art museum, teaching at a community college or coaching a children's sports team. But before you quit your job to pursue these dreams, you should make sure these are indeed the things you want to do—and the best way to find out is to give them a trial run.

INVESTING FOR LIFE

With any luck, I have convinced you to start saving as early as possible in your adult life, so you buy yourself the financial freedom to pursue your passions. But how should you invest those dollars? Consider the story of Ronald Read, who was the subject of a March 2015 article in *The Wall Street Journal*.[38]

"Ronald Read may have spent years pumping gas,

but he was even more adept at pumping up his portfolio," began the article. "Mr. Read, a longtime resident of Brattleboro, Vt., died in June at the age of 92. His friends were shocked when they learned his estate was valued at almost $8 million. Long widowed and with two stepchildren, he left most of his money to a local hospital and library. So how did he manage to pull it off? Besides being a good stock picker, he displayed remarkable frugality and patience—which gave him many years of compounded growth."

It is hard to assess whether Read really was better than average at picking stocks. But he clearly benefited from two other advantages. First, he was extremely frugal, allowing him to save great gobs of money. Second, he lived an exceedingly long time, so he enjoyed years and years of stock market compounding.

Should you also buy stocks? Most folks believe that it makes more sense to buy a home than to rent, because homeowners gradually come to own a valuable asset outright, as they pay down their mortgage. Similarly, given a choice, most people would probably prefer to be an owner of a business, rather than just an employee, because the owner has greater autonomy and makes more money.

The same logic applies when investing. We could lend money, which is what we do when we open a savings account, buy bonds or purchase certificates of deposit. We allow others the use of our money, for which they pay us interest. Alternatively, we could become an owner, which is what happens when we purchase stocks. How can we take full advantage of our extraordinarily long life and hence our extraordinarily long investment time horizon? The answer strikes me as obvious: We should become an owner—by buying a globally diversified stock portfolio.

For many, this suggestion will bring back memories of the horrific 2000–02 and 2007–09 stock market collapses. The first bear market turned $100,000 into $51,000, based on the peak-to-trough price decline for the stocks in the Standard & Poor's 500-index. The second bear market was even worse, shrinking $100,000 to a mere $43,000. These figures exclude the modest benefit we would have gained by reinvesting dividends.

But if we can drag our gaze away from the short-run perils and look at the long-run story, the results are astonishing. Those eye-popping results have been highlighted in the work of Ibbotson Associates, now a unit of Chicago investment researchers Morningstar Inc., and also by Jeremy Siegel, a finance professor at the University of Pennsylvania's Wharton School and author of the 1994 bestseller *Stocks for the Long Run*. Historically, over long holding periods, U.S. stocks have earned 7 percentage points a year more than inflation. Factor in 3 percent inflation and we're looking at a nominal return of 10 percent a year. That is enough to double the value of our money every seven years, thanks to the process of investment compounding, where we earn returns each year not only on our original investment, but also on the gains that we earned in prior years and reinvested back into the market.

To appreciate the fabulous gains that can be generated by long-term investment compounding, try this simple exercise: Input 1,000 into a calculator, representing an initial investment of $1,000. Then multiply this $1,000 by 1.1 again and again. Each time you multiply by 1.1, it increases your $1,000 by 10 percent. That 10 percent is worth just $100 in the first year. But with each passing year, that 10 percent gain translates into a larger dollar amount. When you hit 1.1 for the 50th time, representing the 50th year of investment compounding at 10 percent a year, you add $10,672 to your stash—and your $1,000 initial investment would now be worth $117,391.

TAKING STOCK

Arguably, the amazing long-run return for U.S. stocks is an example of "history as told by the winners." Performance over the past century would look far worse if we considered results for the German, Japanese and Russian stock markets. Arguably, the U.S. stock market's wonderful historical performance also can't be repeated, because it reflects a onetime gain from rising valuations.

Consider two of the most popular measures of the stock market's valuation: the dividend yield and the price-earnings ratio, or P/E. The latter is a company's share price divided by the annual profit that the company is making, with those corporate earnings figured on a per-share basis. At year-end 1915, U.S. stocks had a dividend yield of 4.5 percent and companies were trading at 11 times their earnings for the prior 12 months. By year-end 2015, stocks were much more richly valued, with the dividend yield down to 2.1 percent and stocks trading at a P/E of almost 24.[39] Given today's heady valuations, returns are likely to be significantly lower. But even if we assume far lower returns and even if we assume we aren't lucky enough to invest exclusively in the world's best-performing market, the case for owning stocks is compelling for anyone who has a long time horizon.

Start by pondering the global stock market's performance, as measured by the MSCI World Index, for which data is available going back to year-end 1969. Over the 46 years through year-end 2015, there would have been all kinds of reasons to avoid stocks, including the OPEC oil embargo and skyrocketing inflation of the 1970s, the double-dip recession of the early 1980s, the Dow Jones Industrial Average's 22.6 percent collapse on Oct. 19, 1987, the 1997 Asian currency crisis, the Sept. 11, 2001, terrorist attacks, the 2008–09 financial crisis and more. Yet those who stuck with stocks through all of this would have enjoyed handsome gains. Between year-end 1969 and year-end 2015, the MSCI World Index rose 4,405 percent, enough to turn $10,000 into $450,500, with net dividends reinvested.[40] That 4,405 percent is equal to 8.6 percent a year, while U.S. inflation ran at 4.1 percent.

But let's be cautious and assume annual returns will be lower than 8.6 percent in the years ahead. How much lower? I suspect long-run returns will be around 6 percent a year, while inflation runs at 2 percent. In the pages ahead, I'll explain why. This is probably the most complicated section of the book, but stick with me and I'll try to guide you through.

The stock market's performance can seem baffling to the uninitiated. But it becomes far less mysterious if you break it down into its three component parts: dividend yields, the growth in corporate profits and the price put on those earnings, in the form of the P/E ratio. Vanguard Group founder John C. Bogle uses those three component parts to distinguish between the stock market's "investment" return and its "speculative" return.[41] The investment return consists of the dividend yield plus the growth in corporate earnings per share. Companies can use their growing stream of earnings to boost dividend payments, buy back the company's own shares, expand the business or acquire other businesses.

When we buy stocks, we already know what dividend yield we'll receive. As mentioned above, at year-end 2015, it was roughly 2 percent for the Standard & Poor's 500-stock index. While dividends are occasionally cut, it's fairly safe to assume that owners of the S&P 500 stocks will collect that 2 percent and, indeed, that the dollar amount of dividends paid will grow as corporate profits increase.

What about the growth in earnings per share? That involves a little guesswork. We first need to estimate the U.S. economy's growth rate. Over the 50 years through 2015, the real (after-inflation) GDP growth rate has been 2.9 percent a year. The worst year was a 2.8 percent contraction in 2009 and the best year was a 7.3 percent spurt in 1984. Still, in 37 of the 50 years, growth was between 0 and 5 percent. That's moderately reassuring: It tells us that, most of the time, GDP growth hasn't strayed that far from the 2.9 percent long-run average. Moreover, 10 of the 13 outliers occurred in the first 20 years—and just three in the 30 years since.

The not-so-good news: GDP growth has been slowing over the past 50 years. Since 2000, it has climbed just 1.8 percent a year faster than inflation, on average. Partly, that reflects the Great Recession of 2008–09. But it also reflects slower growth in the labor force. The baby boom generation is leaving the workforce. Younger adults are taking their place, but the new employees barely outnumber those who are departing. Taking that slower growth in the workforce into account, we might assume the economy expands 2 percent a year faster than inflation over the next 10 years. If inflation is also 2 percent, that would put nominal GDP growth at 4 percent.

Will corporate earnings also grow at 4 percent? The economy and earnings growth don't move in lockstep. Corporate profits could grow more slowly if profit margins narrowed or corporate tax rates rose. We also need to factor in international growth. Many U.S. companies do substantial business abroad. If foreign economies are booming, that could help U.S. corporate profits. On the other hand, even if corporate earnings manage to grow at 4 percent a year, earnings figured on a per-share basis will likely grow more slowly, as companies issue new shares to finance their own growth or to compensate employees. Historically, earnings per share have lagged behind overall earnings growth by roughly two percentage points a year, though it may be less in future, because corporations today are more focused on thwarting so-called dilution by repurchasing their own shares.[42]

As you might gather, forecasting corporate earnings growth is a rough-and-ready business. We might assume that earnings will grow at 4 percent, but acknowledge that it could be somewhat faster or slower. Tack on today's 2 percent dividend yield, and we are looking at an estimated 6 percent annual total return for stocks, while inflation runs at 2 percent. This, to use Bogle's expression, is the market's investment return.

SPECULATING ON SPECULATION

For this investment return to be the market's actual

return, share prices would need to climb at 4 percent a year, along with the 4 percent annual growth in earnings per share. Will share prices climb that fast? This is where we get caught up in the market's speculative return. What we are talking about are changes in the value that investors put on corporate earnings, as reflected in the market's price-earnings ratio. If the market's P/E ratio remains the same, share prices would rise at the same rate as corporate earnings, and we would likely get something close to that estimated 6 percent annual total return.

The market's P/E, however, is unlikely to stay the same. Therein lies the dilemma: To come up with an accurate forecast for the stock market's return, we don't just need to know the current dividend yield and estimate how fast corporate earnings will grow. We also need to speculate on how speculative other investors will be. This is the guessing game that consumes all too many investors. We forget about the fundamental value provided by dividend yields and earnings growth, and instead fret endlessly over whether investor sentiment will turn bullish or bearish. We watch every twitch up and down in the Dow Jones Industrial Average, and try to divine what it means for the future.

Economist John Maynard Keynes, writing in the 1930s, likened this speculating on how speculative others would be to the "newspaper competitions in which the competitors have to pick out the six prettiest faces from a hundred photographs, the prize being awarded to the competitor whose choice most nearly corresponds to the average preferences of the competitors as a whole." As Keynes explains, to win the game, "It is not a case of choosing those [faces] which, to the best of one's judgment, are really the prettiest, nor even those which average opinion genuinely thinks the prettiest. We have reached the third degree where we devote our intelligences to anticipating what average opinion expects the average opinion to be."[43]

In the stock market, such madness distracts us from the long-run story and, unfortunately, almost always leaves us poorer. The fact is, if we are long-term investors—and most of us are—the changes in investor sentiment, as reflected in rising and falling P/E ratios, are relatively unimportant. Imagine we are age 20 and looking ahead to age 70, when we might be in the first decade of a lengthy retirement. Or imagine we are age 70, and we are investing money that we plan to bequeath to our 20-year-old granddaughter, who likely won't spend the inheritance until she's retired.

In both cases, we are looking at a 50-year investment time horizon. Let's say we have $10,000 to invest. If we are concerned that investors will turn bearish and P/E ratios will plunge, we might opt for bonds yielding 3 percent. After 50 years, our bonds would be worth some $44,000. Factor in 2 percent inflation over those 50 years, and our $10,000 would grow to just $16,000 in today's dollars. If we also factored in taxes, the final dollar amount would be smaller still.

Now, instead, suppose we bought stocks. At 6 percent a year, our $10,000 would grow to $184,000, or $68,000 after figuring in the corrosive impact of inflation. But what about the risk? Let's assume market valuations were cut in half, so that P/E ratios fell from 20 to 10. Even in that scenario, we would still have $92,000 after 50 years, or almost $34,000 in inflation-adjusted dollars. That's more than double the amount we would have amassed with bonds—and this assumes a collapse in stock market valuations.

Moreover, if there were a collapse in valuations, we could potentially benefit. Most of us don't dump a bunch of money into stocks and then never again invest another dime. Instead, we buy stocks slowly over time, taking a piece of each paycheck and stashing it in our 401(k) plan or sending it off to our favorite mutual fund. If stocks collapsed, we could buy at the cheaper prices and then, assuming there's at least a partial market recovery, we would benefit as shares bounced back.

When I teach personal finance to college students, I include this question on the final exam: "Imagine you're in your 20s and saving every month for retirement. What pattern of market performance would help you accumulate the greatest wealth, assuming stocks had the same cumulative gain over the period?" Students can pick from three answers:

A. High returns now, low returns later

B. Low returns now, high returns later

C. The same return every year

Students invariably get the answer wrong. Most opt for C, in part—I suspect—because they like the idea of earning the same return year after year. But the right answer, of course, is B. For those who have the courage to continue spooning money into the stock market, come what may, a long bear market can be a financial bonanza, because it allows them to scoop up shares at bargain prices.

Don't get me wrong: Nobody should bank

everything on the stock market. If we have money we need to spend in the next five years, it ought to be out of stocks and instead invested in short-term bonds, certificates of deposit, money market funds and savings accounts. But most of our long-term money should be in stocks. The connection between economic growth and share prices may be messy. But they are connected. As long as the economy keeps growing and as long as our time horizon is long enough, we should eventually make decent money. Every so often, our conviction will be tested. At that juncture, we will need to remind ourselves that we are banking not on the short-term fickleness of market sentiment, but on long-run economic growth.

At times when the economy and the markets seem especially grim, it's also worth recalling the apocryphal story of the old trader and the young trader during the 1962 Cuban missile crisis.

Old trader: "They say this could lead to nuclear war."

Young trader: "Then we should buy bonds, right?"

Old trader: "No, we should buy stocks. If this ends peacefully, stocks are going up. And if we have nuclear war, it won't matter what we own."

In late 2008 and early 2009, when the economy and financial markets were teetering on the brink of disaster and many thought the financial world would never be the same again, I would tell myself the story of the old and young trader. If the global economy had collapsed, all financial assets would have suffered, and even owners of bonds and certificates of deposit might have had trouble getting paid. What if the worst didn't come to pass? Stocks would go back up.

LIVING LONG

If we have young children or a spouse who doesn't work, our death could cause major financial problems for our family, which is why we need life insurance. But as the kids grow up and leave home, and as we amass more savings, the financial repercussions of our death become less severe. Instead, as we head toward retirement, we have to grapple with the opposite problem. The risk is no longer that we will die and leave our family in the lurch. Instead, the big financial risk is that we'll live longer than we ever imagined—and run out of money before we run out of breath.

Retirees, however, don't act as though a long life is a major financial risk. Instead, they behave as though death is imminent. This shows up in two key ways. First, consider Social Security retirement benefits. Retirees can claim benefits as early as age 62 or as late as age 70. The longer we delay, the larger our monthly check. Depending on the year we were born, delaying from 62 to 70 can result in an inflation-adjusted benefit that is either 76 or 77 percent larger.

Among those claiming Social Security retirement benefits in 2014, 43 percent of men and 49 percent of women were age 62, the youngest possible age. These figures exclude those on disability benefits who were automatically converted over to receive retirement benefits.[44] By claiming benefits in the first year they are eligible, retirees will receive their monthly check for more years, but the size of their benefit will be permanently reduced. A smart move? Suppose we compare claiming Social Security at age 62 to claiming benefits at age 66 or even age 70, which would give us a larger monthly check but for fewer years.

To make the comparison, let's assume we plan to

collect our Social Security benefit and invest it in something of similar risk. The obvious alternative would be high-quality bonds, which also provide a steady, relatively low-risk stream of income. If we claim benefits early, we can begin buying bonds earlier. If we delay, we get off to a slower start with our bond purchases, but we will be able to invest more each month.

When does starting later put us ahead of the game? It depends on the rate of return we can earn by buying bonds. If we assume returns are 1 or 2 percentage points a year better than inflation, which is what we can usually get with high-quality bonds, we should come out ahead by delaying benefits if we live until our early 80s. That is younger than the life expectancy for the typical U.S. retiree and well below the life expectancy for affluent Americans. Moreover, even if we die young, our Social Security benefit may live on, thanks to the survivor benefit that could be paid to our spouse. The implication: By rushing to claim Social Security at age 62, most retirees are hurting themselves financially.

That brings us to the second indicator that retirees are more concerned with an early death than a long life: In 2015, just $9.1 billion was invested in immediate fixed annuities, according to the LIMRA Secure Retirement Institute. That might sound like a big number. But it's a drop in the bucket compared to other financial products. For instance, $230.9 billion flooded into exchange-traded funds in 2015, calculates the Investment Company Institute. Like Social Security, an immediate fixed annuity can provide retirees with lifetime income. We hand over a lump sum to an insurance company, which then cuts us a check every month for the rest of our life. Again, this is not unlike buying a bond, but with some key differences. A bond pays interest for a fixed period of time, at which point we get back the sum originally invested in the bond, otherwise known as the bond's principal value. An income annuity typically has no principal value, but it generates more annual income—and the issuing insurance company guarantees that this income will be paid for as long as we live.

Like the idea of guaranteed lifetime income? There's an intriguing, and relatively new, variant on immediate fixed annuities known as longevity insurance. We might buy longevity insurance at, say, age 65. But instead of paying us income right away, longevity insurance starts paying us lifetime income only if we live to a particular age, such as 80 or 85. It's like buying an immediate fixed annuity, except it's cheaper, because you don't get income in the early years. An immediate fixed annuity might be viewed as a bond with a little insurance attached, in case we live beyond our life expectancy. By contrast, longevity insurance (sometimes also called a deferred income annuity) can be seen as pure insurance, allowing us to hedge the risk that we will live a surprisingly long time and start to deplete our savings. Keep in mind that, in both cases, buyers are betting that the insurance company will be around to make the promised payments, so it's wise to stick with insurers that have a top rating for financial strength, while also hedging our bets by buying annuities from a variety of insurers.

Immediate fixed annuities and longevity insurance are a way to share risk with other retirees. If we live to our late 80s and beyond, we will continue to receive monthly income from these products, with our checks effectively subsidized by other annuity buyers who died earlier in retirement. This sort of risk pooling is a great way to handle life's financial pitfalls, and we are reasonably happy to do it—most of the time. When we buy life insurance or we purchase a homeowner's policy, we are contributing to a pool of money managed by an insurance company and to which many others are contributing. Those who see their homes burn down, and the families of those who die, collect big money from the pool. Those who remain standing—and whose homes remain standing—don't collect on their insurance policies. They paid their premiums and got nothing in return, but you won't hear many complaints.

Unless, that is, we are talking about a form of risk pooling known as an immediate fixed annuity. Why do folks—who happily buy life, health, disability, auto and other insurance—balk at this type of risk pooling? Why do retirees rush to claim Social Security as soon as they are eligible? Over the years, I have heard all kinds of explanations. Retirees tell me they claimed Social Security right away because they fear the system will collapse or because they believe that they can earn some outrageously high return by investing their monthly benefit. Others tell me they avoid immediate fixed annuities because annuities have a bad reputation. That deservedly bad reputation, however, belongs to variable annuities and equity-indexed annuities, which are radically different products, involving far higher costs and far greater complexity.

While retirees offer a host of reasons for not buying immediate fixed annuities and not delaying Social Security, their widely differing objections often have a common underlying theme: They just aren't comfortable with a financial bet that hinges on living a long life. Perhaps this reflects our tendency to focus on the days and weeks ahead, while shortchanging next year and beyond—the same shortsightedness that prompts us to panic when long-term investments suffer short-term declines and causes us to spend too much today and save too little for the future. Perhaps, thanks to our ancient instincts, we are hardwired to assume that life will be nasty, brutish and short. Perhaps we are hardwired to worry about our offspring's well-being. We can't bear the thought that we will buy annuities and delay Social Security, and then suffer an early death and leave less to our heirs. Or maybe it's some combination of these things: If we die early in retirement, not only will we fail to get much back from our big annuity investment and from Social Security, but also we will be well and truly dead—and that thought just isn't palatable.

Whatever the reason, this is an instinct worth fighting. By avoiding immediate annuities and claiming Social Security early, we are failing to exploit one of the great financial advantages that we all share. What advantage? Our life expectancy may be vastly improved—but we won't live forever. Looking at life more broadly, this might seem like a mixed blessing. But from a financial point of view, our eventual mortality is a big winner, and we can use it to our benefit.

By delaying Social Security while tapping other savings to cover our living costs during our early retirement years, we can lock in a far larger stream of inflation-adjusted income. Why is the federal government willing to cut us a much larger monthly check, in return for waiting just a handful of years? The government knows we are that much closer to death and thus, on average, the government might only have to cut those checks for perhaps 20 years, rather than 25. That larger stream of income can make for a more comfortable and less financially stressful retirement. My contention: If you're a single individual in good health, or you're married and you were the family's main breadwinner, delaying Social Security benefits until age 70 should be a top financial priority.

I am not willing to bang the table quite so hard for income annuities. Compared to delaying Social Security, the financial payoff isn't as attractive, plus buyers are betting that the insurance company won't go bust. But if you have delayed Social Security to get the maximum possible benefit and you want yet more guaranteed income, immediate fixed annuities and longevity insurance could make sense.

Even if you aren't inclined to buy immediate fixed annuities, they offer a powerful illustration of the financial advantage conferred by our eventual death. Think about it this way: If we are unwilling to annuitize, we have to save enough to cover our living costs for however long we might live. Given the uncertainty, we should probably make sure we're financially prepared to live until at least age 95. What if we are willing to annuitize? To generate the same amount of retirement income, we don't need to save nearly so much. The reason: An insurance company will sell us an annuity based on the notion that we and other annuitants will, as a group, live until our late 80s. What if we live longer? The insurance company will pick up the tab.

STEP NO. 3:

REWIRE YOUR BRAIN

We Are Hardwired for Financial Failure—
So Sensible Money Management Takes
Great Mental Strength

M ost of us make all kinds of financial errors: We spend too much and save too little. We take on too much debt. We panic when the stock market goes down. We grow too bold with our investment bets as share prices climb. Why are we so messed up? Forget blaming our parents. Instead, we should probably blame our great, great, great, great, great-grandparents—our hunter-gatherer ancestors.

Cast your mind back 10,000 years or so to the time before humans settled down and started cultivating crops and domesticating animals. What were our nomadic ancestors like? We are here today because they survived and reproduced. Many others lost the battle for survival, but our ancestors didn't. What qualities did they possess? We don't know for sure.

But we can make an educated guess: They likely consumed whenever they could, because tomorrow there might be no food. They imitated others, because following the crowd was how they learned how to survive. They were constantly looking for patterns, such as signs that food and water were nearby or hints that the weather was changing. They reacted swiftly to any whiff of danger, whether it was the threat from a predator or a possible shortage of food, because such perils could mean extinction. They were fiercely protective of their families and others in their tribe, because by banding together they and their offspring were more likely to survive, thus ensuring that the family line continued. They worked hard, were relentless in their efforts to secure food and shelter, and were never satisfied with what they had, because any slacking off could imperil survival.

And you and I aren't a whole lot different.

In some quarters, references to evolutionary psychology raise hackles, because of the suggestion that we are merely puppets controlled by our genes and that we don't have free will. I would favor a more nuanced view. Yes, we are hardwired to behave in certain ways. But that doesn't mean we always follow our instincts. We can buck our natural inclinations—and often, when managing money, that's the right thing to do. But we shouldn't kid ourselves: This takes great mental effort.

MAKING MISTAKES

Chapter 1 discussed how we fail to get the most out

of our money, because we aren't very good at figuring out what will make us happy. Chapter 2 pointed out that most of us will live an extraordinarily long life, and yet we don't factor that into our financial behavior. These are hardly our only errors.

Below, you will read about 22 mental mistakes that have been identified by experts in behavioral finance.[45] Running such a lengthy list might seem like overkill. But if we're to be successful managers of our own money, we need to come to grips with some unflattering truths. We're ill-disciplined, including spending too much, taking on too much debt and saving too little. We're incapable of forecasting the market's short-term direction (and even long-term predictions are a dodgy business), and yet we regularly buy and sell based on these useless forecasts. Over a lifetime of investing, we will almost certainly fail to pick investments that outperform the market averages. But with brazen self-confidence, we keep on trying.

Many of the errors identified by researchers relate to saving and investing, with fewer on topics such as buying homes, claiming Social Security and taking on debt. That doesn't mean we behave any more sensibly in these other areas of our financial life. Rather, it reflects the availability of data. The stock market sees billions of shares traded every day, making it a playground for number-crunching academics. Other areas of personal finance don't offer quite the same numerical cornucopia.

As you read the list below, you might spot mistakes that friends and family make—and you may recognize some of your own behavior. Not everybody makes all of the mistakes listed. But these mental mistakes are sufficiently pervasive and enduring that they can't be dismissed as the errors of an irrational few. Hard as we might try, none of us behaves like the dispassionate, rational *homo economicus* assumed by traditional economic theory. Want to improve your money management? Here are 22 errors that stand in your way:

1. *We're too focused on the short-term.* Experts keep advising us to save and invest, so we can retire in 20 or 30 years. And yet we remain almost exclusively focused on the here and now. Is there a new toy we're hankering to buy? To persuade us to postpone the purchase for a mere 12 months, somebody would likely have to offer us a huge financial incentive.

   We are also overly influenced by recent events, including the latest political news, the current crop of economic data, and whether the financial markets have lately been rising or falling. We ascribe great importance to the days and weeks ahead, and not nearly enough to next year, let alone the next 10 years.

2. *We lack self-control.* America's miserably low savings rate partly stems from our short-term focus. But it also reflects our lack of self-control. Our ancestors didn't have to worry about restraining their consumption so they could amass money for retirement. We, alas, do need self-control. But for most of us, it is a lifelong struggle.

3. *We believe the secret to investment success is hard work.* Activity, we figure, will bring success, whether it is diligently reading corporate annual reports or trading rapidly throughout the day. While all this activity might give us the illusion of control over

our investment results, it is more likely to hurt our performance, as we rack up hefty trading costs and make large undiversified investment bets.

4. *We think the future is predictable.* In retrospect, it seems obvious that technology stocks were going to crash and burn after the huge run-up of the late 1990s. Similarly, we aren't surprised that the housing bubble of the early 2000s burst. In fact, we are pretty sure we foresaw both market collapses.

   Did we? At issue is a phenomenon known as hindsight bias. We forget about all the uncertainty that existed at the time and all the predictions we made that turned out wrong. Thanks to our sanitized recollection of the past, we feel future events are more predictable than they really are— and this can prompt us to make big investment bets that we later regret.

5. *We see patterns where none exists.* When we are struck by some sudden shift in the market's direction or we learn about a new company, we hunt for analogies. We might think, "It's 1999 all over again," as we watch stocks climb by leaps and bounds and we worry about another bear market. We might imagine, "It's the next Apple," if we come across a company with a hot new technology product.

   As financial markets bounce up and down, we also tend to either extrapolate recent returns or expect a reversal. Those who extrapolate will assume that rising markets will continue to rise, prompting them to invest more, and that falling markets will keep plunging, which might cause them to panic and sell. Meanwhile, those who expect a reversal might rush to buy during down markets and rush to sell when prices rise.

6. *We hate losing.* Studies suggest that the pain we get from losses is more than twice as great as the pleasure we receive from gains. Suppose we were offered the chance to bet $100 on a coin flip. If we called heads or tails incorrectly, we would lose our $100. To entice us to play, how much would winning need to be worth?

A $100 prize would make it a fair bet. Yet, to induce most of us to play, it would likely take $200 or more—an indication of just how much we hate losing money. This distaste for losses helps explain why investors have, historically, shied away from stocks, despite the handsome long-run gains.

7. *We sell winners and hang on to losers.* While investors are often described as risk averse, it's more accurate to say we are loss averse. When faced with a loss, we might take additional risk in an effort to recoup the loss, such as buying more shares if one of our stocks falls in value. This is sometimes referred to as "doubling down."

Our goal: to get even, before we get out. We might refuse to sell until an investment gets back to our purchase price, or gets close enough that we can tell ourselves that we have broken even. This isn't just about losing money. It's also about losing face. If we hang on, we can comfort ourselves with the thought that "it's only a paper loss." Selling would force us to admit we made a mistake, with all the associated pangs of regret. Often, however, the smarter strategy is to take the loss, especially if we hold the shares in a taxable account, because we can then use the loss to reduce our income tax bill.

Even as we hang on to losers, we often rush to sell our winners. Why? It may simply be pride. It feels good when we realize our gains and turn them into cash, even though selling can trigger trading costs and also a big tax bill if the stock is held in a taxable account.

8. *We're overconfident.* Most of us believe we are better-than-average drivers, more intelligent than most people, and also better looking. This isn't necessarily a bad trait. Optimistic, confident people tend to be happier, they cope better with stress and they are more likely to succeed at their chosen profession.

    But the reality is that, unlike the children of Garrison Keillor's Lake Wobegon, we can't all be better than average. Our excessive self-confidence is a real handicap when it comes to investing. It encourages us to trade too much, to believe that we can beat the market and to make large, undiversified investment bets.

9. *We take credit for our winners, while blaming our losers on others.* If we buy an investment and it goes up, it was our brilliant choice. If it goes down, it's the fault of our broker, or those clowns in Washington, or that idiot on television we listened to. This delusional reaction to winning and losing reduces the chances that we will learn from our mistakes, while further bolstering our self-confidence.

    It also helps to explain the bandwagon effect we see during rising markets. As stocks climb, more and more investors make money, pumping up their confidence and making them even more willing to take risk. This growing appetite for risk receives additional fuel from the so-called house money effect. Like casino gamblers who get lucky early in the evening, we start to feel like we are ahead of the game, prompting us to take even more risk.

10. *Our risk tolerance isn't stable.* When building an investment portfolio, we are often advised to think about how much risk we can stomach, and then use that to guide how much we put in stocks and how much in bonds. The problem: Our risk tolerance isn't stable, so the portfolio we are happy to own today may make us miserable a year from now.

Why does our appetite for risk change? At issue are many of the mental mistakes mentioned above. When the stock market falls, we might extrapolate the decline and sell shares in a panic. Alternatively, we might put even more into stocks, because we expect the market decline to reverse or because the prospect of losing money prompts us to double down on stocks in an effort to recoup our losses.

What about when markets rise? We might sell because we enjoy realizing gains or because we expect a reversal—or we might throw even more money into the market because we imagine "the trend is our friend." We might also be tempted to stash more in stocks because of the house money effect.

11. *We get anchored to particular prices.* Suppose we heard that our neighbors' home sold two years ago for $300,000. We might decide that our home should sell for at least that much—even if property prices

have fallen during the intervening two years. Alternatively, we might own a stock that once got as high as $50, but which has since fallen to $30. We might be stuck on that $50 price and refuse to sell for less.

12. *We rationalize bad decisions.* Instead of acknowledging and then correcting a mistake, we will often cook up stories to make our bad decision seem more rational. We might even change our recollection of the decision, so we recall behaving more sensibly than we did. The unease we feel is sometimes referred to as cognitive dissonance. To escape the discomfort, we try to resolve two contradictory thoughts. The notion that "I just made a stupid financial decision" might clash with the idea that "I'm smart about handling money," and we try to find some way to make the stupid financial decision seem more intelligent.

13. *We favor familiar investments.* This might include shares of our employer, companies that compete in the industry where we work, corporations that are headquartered near our home and companies whose products we use. The familiarity makes these stocks more comfortable to own, but the result is often a badly diversified portfolio with a lot of unnecessary risk.

14. *We put a higher value on investments we already own.* This is known as the endowment effect. Why do we endow some investments with additional value, which then makes us reluctant to sell? Maybe it's the familiarity. Maybe it's a sense of commitment that comes with picking out an investment and then putting our dollars behind it. Maybe we

bought based on the recommendation of somebody we like or we inherited the investment from our parents, so we have an emotional attachment.

15. *We prefer sins of omission to sins of commission.* If we fail to sell a stock and the shares subsequently fall in price, we might kick ourselves. But our sense of regret will likely be less than if we did go ahead and sell—and soon after the shares skyrocketed in value. This fear that our actions may make matters worse is sometimes referred to as "status quo bias."

16. *We find stories more convincing than statistics.* Academic studies tell us that value stocks—those shares that are cheap based on market yardsticks like price-earnings ratios and dividend yield—outperform growth stocks, despite the latter's rapidly increasing earnings and sales. But academic studies are no competition for a good story: We are still drawn to hot growth companies with their slick innovations and adoring customers.

Growth stocks also offer the chance to dream: We can imagine that the stock might suddenly soar 100 or 200 percent. In fact, the anticipation is often more enjoyable than actually making money. It's not unlike vacations, where imagining where we might go is frequently more fun than the actual trip. On top of that, hot growth stocks offer a payoff structure we find appealing: As with lottery tickets, the investment is modest compared to the potential gain—even if, most of the time, we come away empty-handed.

17. *We base decisions on information that's easily recalled.* Airplane crashes make the news, so we are more

fearful of flying than driving, even though car accidents cause many more deaths. Similarly, we hear a lot about investment legend Warren Buffett and a lot about lottery ticket winners, which makes beating the market and winning the lottery seem far more likely than they really are.

18. *We latch onto information that confirms what we already believe.* At the same time, we discount information that contradicts our beliefs. This is a common phenomenon among those who are bullish or bearish on the stock market. The bulls spy reasons for optimism everywhere they look. What about the bears? They see just the opposite.

   Along these lines, I recall receiving dueling letters from *Wall Street Journal* readers. One pointed out the large gap for most stocks between their highest and lowest share price over the past year. He argued that this was proof that it was easy to make money in the stock market. The other reader pointed out the same phenomenon—and said it proved how easy it was to lose money.

19. *We believe there's safety in numbers.* Purchasing investments that "everybody's buying" can make investing seem less frightening. But often, it isn't good for our investment returns. While popularity may be a useful guide when picking a restaurant or choosing a movie, it can be a disaster when investing, because we can find ourselves buying overpriced investments.

20. *Our financial decisions aren't purely financial.* Like ordinary consumer purchases, financial choices have three benefits: utilitarian (what it does for me), expressive (what it says about me) and

emotional (how it makes me feel). As we manage our finances, we might insist our goal is strictly utilitarian, and that all we want to do is make money. But in truth, we often make decisions for expressive or emotional reasons, and these other motivations can hurt our stated goal of greater wealth.

We might be proud to own a hedge fund or use a private money manager, despite the high fees that make it unlikely we will earn market-beating returns. We might feel good about investing in a mutual fund that buys companies that are socially responsible. We might get a thrill from rapidly trading stocks. This trading can also lead to a state of "flow," mentioned in chapter 2. We become pleasantly immersed in rapidly buying and selling shares, even as all this trading hurts us financially. Similarly, we might get a thrill from buying growth stocks and initial public stock offerings, both of which offer the chance to dream of an exceptionally large payoff.[46]

21. *We engage in mental accounting.* This shows up in three key ways. First, we divvy up our wealth into different mental buckets, and view each bucket differently. For instance, we might happily spend money in our checking account, but we are reluctant to sell any of our mutual funds, unless it's a dire emergency.

Second, we might pay heed to the experts and build a diversified portfolio. But instead of focusing on our overall portfolio's performance, we waste the emotional benefit that comes with broad diversification by fretting over the results of each investment we own.

Third, we may make a sharp distinction between money derived from investment income and money from selling our holdings. Remember the old adages about "never spend your capital" and "never dip into principal"? Along those lines, retirees will often happily spend their dividends and interest, but they are reluctant to sell any of their stocks and bonds. This mindset can lead retirees to buy high-yielding investments—and end up taking more risk than they realize.

22. *We're influenced by how issues are framed.* Many 401(k) plans no longer ask employees whether they want to contribute. Instead, they ask employees if they want to opt out of participating. If we were rational, it wouldn't matter how the question was framed. But in this case, it produces a radically different outcome. By asking employees if they want to opt out, 401(k) plans tap into our tendency toward inertia and make participation appear to be the norm. Result: Many more employees put away money for retirement.

Similarly, we can be influenced by how investment gains and losses are framed. We might be told that, "over the past 50 years, stocks have made money in 75 percent of all calendar years." Alternatively, we might be told that "over the past 50 years, stocks have lost money in 25 percent of all calendar years." The two sentences tell us the same thing—yet the first description makes stocks seem more appealing.

Another classic example: If people are asked if they are in a relationship and then asked if they are happy, those who are in a relationship are more likely to say they are happy. But if people aren't asked the relationship question, the gap in reported happiness isn't nearly so wide between those who are in a relationship and those who aren't.

SAVING LIKE CRAZY

Like the research on money and happiness, the insights from behavioral finance are compelling— because they ring true. When we stop and think about it, we see how shaky the connection is between money and happiness. Similarly, as rational as we like to think we are, we also know the stock market's turmoil plays with our heads and we know we often spend far more than we planned.

How can we keep ourselves on the straight and narrow? While experts have uncovered an astonishing array of mental mistakes, three strike me as especially problematic. First, we lack self-control, which means we tend to overspend and take on too much debt. Second, we have too much confidence in our investment abilities, leading us to trade too much, buy actively managed funds and make large investment bets, as we try to notch market-beating gains. But that confidence is easily shaken, which brings us to the third problem: We are too quick to change our minds when markets tumble, in part because we are so averse to losing money.

How can we overcome these traits and rewire our brains, so we succeed financially? I believe we need to squelch our instincts and strive to acquire three financial habits, none of which comes easily: We need to turn ourselves into great savers, we need humility and we need to train ourselves to focus on the stock market's fundamental value. The rest of this chapter is devoted to these three crucial attributes.

The first is the most important. Even if we have the tenacity to stick with a sensible investment strategy in the face of market turmoil, our investment gains won't amount to much in dollar terms unless we have a decent sum invested in the market—and that takes good savings habits.

Those habits don't come naturally. When my kids were young, we would often take walks around the neighborhood. They would see big homes with manicured lawns, and his and her luxury European sedans sitting in the driveway, and they would exclaim, "Wow, they must be rich." As Hannah and Henry rolled their eyes, I would climb onto the parental soapbox: "That doesn't mean they have a lot of money. It means they spent a lot of money." I would then point out that the mansion might be heavily mortgaged, the cars might be leased and the landscaper might still be awaiting payment.

We associate wealth with outward displays of opulence. But this is yet another instance when our instincts fail us. Over the decades, both at *The Wall Street Journal* and at Citigroup, I have met and corresponded with thousands of ordinary Americans who have amassed seven-figure portfolios. Many of these folks had relatively modest salaries. Most were mediocre investors. But almost all shared one key attribute: They were extremely frugal, otherwise known as cheap. Our wealthiest neighbors are often the family with the modest house and the second-hand cars. They have heaps of money because they aren't big spenders, and instead live far beneath their means and save diligently.

This was the thesis of the 1996 bestselling book *The Millionaire Next Door*, written by Thomas Stanley and

William Danko.[47] The book was an eye-opener for many, and the phrase "the millionaire next door" became shorthand for describing a surprisingly wealthy slice of American society and yet one that's almost invisible. Unless we get a peek at their financial statements, we would have no idea how rich these folks are. The many everyday millionaires I have met are skeptical that more possessions will make their life better—and bemused that their fellow citizens' self-esteem seems to hinge on wearing designer clothes and owning the latest electronic gadget.

Stanley, who died in 2015, subsequently wrote another book, *Stop Acting Rich…And Start Living Like a Real Millionaire*.[48] In that 2009 book, he included a series of statistics about the spending habits of those with $1 million or more in investable assets:

- Never owned a boat: 70 percent
- Never owned a vacation home: 64 percent
- Most popular car based on latest purchase: Toyota
- Median price paid for dinner at the restaurant they frequent most often: $20
- Median price paid for a man's haircut: $16
- Median price paid for a bottle of wine when having guests over: $13[49]

As Stanley made clear, the secret to getting rich is no secret at all: We need to be great savers. But while growing wealthy is ridiculously simple, it isn't easy. The annual savings rate over the decade through year-end 2015 averaged just 5.1 percent of disposable personal income. The battle between our current self and our future self turns out to be a one-sided fight: We overwhelmingly favor today. How can we level the playing field, so our future self has a fighting chance?

There are all kinds of rational reasons to be a good saver: By socking away money early and often, we can avoid a lifetime of financial anxiety, enjoy decades of investment compounding, buy ourselves the financial freedom to pursue our passions and ensure a comfortable retirement. Meanwhile, as we learned in chapter 1, spending less today isn't any great sacrifice, because much of our spending delivers little happiness.

Appeals to rationality, however, are no match for our lack of self-control and our instinct to consume as much as possible today. What to do? Consider a two-part strategy. First, we should make it possible to save by keeping our fixed living costs as low as possible. We're talking here about recurring expenses such as mortgage or rent, car payments, groceries, utilities and insurance premiums. In particular, we should focus on the sum we devote to housing and cars, because together those two items account for half of the typical American family's spending. If these and other fixed costs are too high, we won't be able to save much, no matter how much we want to. Many Americans would love to save more, I suspect, but they simply can't— because they have boxed themselves in with high fixed living costs. My advice: Aim to keep your total fixed costs below 50 percent of pretax income.

Second, we should make saving as painless as possible. That means signing up to contribute to our employer's 401(k) or 403(b) plan, so the money gets pulled from our paycheck before we get a chance to spend it. This is the classic way to "pay yourself first." If we want to save more than our 401(k) allows, or our employer doesn't offer a retirement plan, we could arrange to invest automatically every month in one or two mutual funds, with the money pulled directly from our checking account.

We might also pay off the mortgage more quickly by rounding up the monthly check to the nearest $100, so the $1,623 mortgage payment becomes $1,700. We might make a point of saving all windfalls, such as tax refunds, income from freelance work, insurance reimbursements and year-end bonuses. These sums aren't part of our regular income, so they should be a painless source of extra savings.

Soon enough, these habits will become ingrained and the financial benefits will start to snowball. Our portfolio will balloon and our sense of financial control will grow. We will also enjoy three benefits that aren't widely appreciated. First, if we keep our fixed costs low, not only will we have more money to save, but also we will have more money for discretionary spending like eating out, vacations and fun experiences such as concerts and amusement parks—all likely to deliver ample happiness.

Second, if we're used to living far below our means, we will need a far smaller nest egg to retire in comfort. One rule of thumb says that, in retirement, we need income equal to 80 percent of our final salary. But if we regularly save 25 percent of our income, rather than the often recommended 10 percent, we're used to living on a relatively small portion of our paycheck—and we might be able to retire comfortably on just 65 percent of our preretirement income.

Third, by being frugal early in our adult life, we will enjoy the pleasure of a gradually rising standard of living. If we start out in economy but eventually we can afford to fly first class, sitting at the front of the plane will seem like a treat. What if we start out in first class? It won't seem all that special—and, when our skimpy retirement nest egg forces us to the back of the plane, sitting in the cheap seats will seem especially grim.

EMBRACING HUMILITY

It's the great Wall Street fantasy: With hard work, street smarts and maybe a little luck, we can pick the right stocks and mutual funds, and thereby beat the market. This fantasy is so powerful that it sustains an entire industry—one that encompasses investment newsletters, professional money managers, financial websites, cable business channels, market strategists, securities analysts, boutique investment research firms, financial talk radio shows and more. These folks are desperate to keep the fantasy alive, because their livelihoods depend on it.

Yet the fantasy should have died decades ago. Before the 1970s, institutional and individual investors simply assumed that their money managers beat the market. If they bothered to compare their portfolios to a market index, it was often to the price change for shares in the Dow Jones Industrial Average. That meant dividends were excluded, which historically have accounted for almost half the market's total return. "Any sort of performance measurement, as we think of it today, was extremely primitive," the late Peter Bernstein, an economist and bestselling author, told me for a 1996 article. "We had portfolios in which everybody owned bonds, and we compared them to the Dow Jones average, which was ridiculous. But nobody told us it was ridiculous."[50]

Three developments converged to explode the myth that professional money managers regularly beat the market. First, many money managers had atrocious performance during the 1973–74 bear market, in large part because they were overweighted in the "nifty fifty" growth stocks that got hit hard in the market collapse. Second, improved technology made it easier to calculate the returns for market indexes, notably the Standard & Poor's 500-stock index, so investors had a better sense for how their managers stacked up against the market. Third, and perhaps most important, investors and academics started looking more closely at the audited, publicly available performance for a select group of money managers—those who ran mutual funds. Private money managers have long played games with their results by excluding the performance of some accounts or not deducting their management fee, thus making their returns look better than they really were. As Wall Street professionals often wryly note, every money manager somehow claims to be top quartile.

But mutual funds find it harder to hide from scrutiny. Yes, the data can suffer from so-called survivorship bias, as rotten-performing funds are closed down or merged into other funds, thus causing their records to conveniently disappear. Yes, there are incubator funds, which are opened up to the public if they perform well—and quietly killed off if they don't. But even with those problems, funds have long been a ready source of data for academics. An obvious research question: Are money managers delivering on their boasts of market-beating performance? The answer turned out to be a resounding "no." An early academic study analyzed fund performance between 1945 and 1964.[51] As a group, the 115 funds studied didn't outperform a strategy of merely buying and holding the stocks in a market index, and that held true even if fund performance was analyzed with each fund's operating expenses added back. To be sure, some of the 115 funds performed well. But their results were no better than you would have expected based on chance.

As the evidence mounted that most mutual funds performed poorly, interest in index funds grew among both individual and institutional investors, with the first index mutual fund launched by Vanguard Group in 1976. Index funds simply purchase many or all of the securities that make up a market index, in an effort to replicate the index's performance. The funds almost always fall short of that goal, because of the investment costs they incur. But because most index funds charge such low costs, the shortfall is typically modest, and certainly far less than that suffered by most actively managed funds, with their significantly higher annual expenses.

For years, private money managers and others heaped scorn on index funds, while also claiming that actively managed mutual funds weren't representative of the money-management business, because mutual funds were run by second-rate stock pickers. These arguments didn't hold up. Many pension funds, endowments and other institutional investors took a close look at their stable of money managers, realized they weren't delivering the goods and opted to index instead. Individual investors reached similar conclusions: Index funds—both the mutual-fund variety and those that are listed on the exchanges— have attracted trillions of dollars in recent years, as everyday investors have turned their back on actively managed funds. What about those private money managers, who were supposedly so much cleverer than their mutual-fund counterparts? Many subsequently launched their own mutual funds—and their results proved just as mediocre.

If you want a reality check, take a look at the study that's regularly put out by S&P Dow Jones Indices, part of McGraw Hill Financial. The study is known as the SPIVA Scorecard, short for Standard & Poor's Indices Versus Active. It compares actively managed funds to appropriate benchmark indexes. Over a 10-year period, typically 20 percent or less of actively managed funds outperform their category's benchmark index.[52] To the excessively self-confident, a one-in-five chance of outperforming the market might not sound so terrible.

But anyone hoping for market-beating gains faces an added headache. Yes, the history books tell us who won in the past. But they don't tell us who will win in the future. Suppose you picked stock funds that ranked in their category's top 25 percent over the past five years. Another regularly updated study from S&P Dow Jones Indices suggests that less than a quarter of these funds will remain in the top 25 percent over the next five years—even worse than the result you would expect based purely on chance.[53] Past performance truly is no guarantee of future results.

For many investors, all of this is hard to swallow. Faced with the uncertainty of the market, they want that sense of control that comes with actively managing their money. They feel sure they can spot the winners and figure out which way the market is headed next. They are confident they can succeed, because they are smarter and harder working than others. They can't bring themselves to accept that the future is unknowable and that they should simply diversify broadly, buy index funds and let their money ride.

And yet that is what we should do. The logic of

investing is brutal: Before costs, investors collectively earn the market's return. After costs, we must—as a group—lag behind. In fact, we collectively trail the market by an amount equal to the investment costs we incur. A minority of active investors will get lucky and beat the market this year. But it's highly unlikely that we will be lucky over a lifetime of investing. If we actively manage our portfolio in an effort to outperform the market averages, we will incur annual costs equal to perhaps 2 percent of our portfolio's value—and that's the amount by which we are likely to trail the market each year over the long haul.

The alternative: Buy a globally diversified portfolio of stock and bond index funds, and then collect the market's return, minus a modest loss to investment costs. While active investors lag behind the market by an average 2 percentage points a year, indexers might trail by just 0.1 percentage point. By buying and holding index funds, we are guaranteed to beat our neighbors—but we also give up all chance of beating the market. This may not seem terribly exciting. But investing isn't meant to be exciting. It's meant to be profitable.

As investors, we shouldn't aim to beat the market, prove how clever we are or become the richest family in town. Instead, the objective is to amass enough to pay for the house down payment, the kids' college and our own retirement. Abandoning efforts to beat the market, and instead sitting humbly and quietly with a diverse collection of index funds, will give us a far better shot at achieving those goals. The meek may not inherit the earth, but they are far more likely to retire in comfort.

FINDING VALUE

When we buy a stock or a mutual fund, we are betting that it will be worth more at some point in the future. The moment of purchase is one of great hope. Who knows how much we might make? Reality, however, quickly intrudes. Investing can be seen as a battle between two competing pieces of information: what we think an investment is worth—and what the market says.

The market, unfortunately, has the upper hand. It bullies and seduces, often prompting us to change our minds. As the broad stock market rises, our expectations are nudged higher and we imagine our stocks and mutual funds will soon be worth far more than we had previously hoped. When shares tumble, we are thrown into doubt, as we ponder whether the stocks we just bought might be worth significantly less than we thought. The gyrating prices mess with our head, our confidence ebbs and flows, our fear of losses is ignited and we imagine we can see patterns in the market's erratic price movements.

Once again, all of this can be blamed on our Pleistocene brain. In the ancient world, imitating others was how we learned to survive. Spotting patterns helped us to hunt for animals, detect weather changes and figure out when it was time to migrate. A fear of losses allowed us to avoid deadly missteps. Working hard helped ensure that we had enough food and that our offspring survived.

But in the modern financial world, these virtues become vices. Working hard can lead us to trade too much and incur substantial investment costs, as we strive for market-beating gains we are unlikely to achieve. Imitating others can cause us to buy popular, overpriced investments. Searching for patterns can lead us to believe we know what will happen next in the markets, when in truth all we're observing are random price movements. Our fear of losses can cause us to make panicky decisions when share prices tumble.

To avoid this maelstrom of emotions, investors are sometimes told to ignore short-term market fluctuations. That is tough to do—and it may not be smart. Market prices, which reflect the collective judgment of millions of investors, are often a good indicator of value. The vast majority of money managers, who devote their professional life to scouring the markets, aren't skilled enough at finding undervalued investments to overcome the trading costs they incur and the management fees they charge, and thereby deliver market-beating returns. That suggests that, much of the time, stocks, bonds and other investments are indeed fairly priced.

This contention underpins the efficient market hypothesis. I don't subscribe to the strong version of the hypothesis, which says securities are always correctly priced. But I believe the market is sufficiently efficient that it is extraordinarily hard for investors to earn market-beating returns over the long run, and thus most of us should avoid actively managed funds and steer clear of picking individual stocks. What if we dabble in individual stocks and one of them plunges in price? The market is telling us that something is amiss and maybe we have ourselves a dud.

STAYING GROUNDED

This conflating of price and value, however, has its dangers. Think back to March 2009, when the Standard

& Poor's 500-stock index was 57 percent below its October 2007 high. If we had bought a collection of stocks for $1,000 and then came to believe that their true value was just $430, dumping our holdings wouldn't have been an unreasonable response. After all, given the huge loss in just 17 months, who knew what our shares might be worth if we stuck with them for another few months?

But selling in March 2009 would, of course, have been a terrible mistake—which is why we need a sense of stocks' value that is distinct from their price. As investors' emotions run wild, it seems the stock market occasionally overshoots, with share prices becoming far too cheap or far too expensive. In his 1949 classic *The Intelligent Investor*, author Benjamin Graham told the parable of the manic-depressive Mr. Market, who is your partner in business and every day tells you what he thinks your share of the business is worth. You might take Mr. Market up on his offer, and buy or sell at the price he's quoting. But you shouldn't let his latest price be the sole determinant of what you think your stocks are worth.[54]

Admittedly, if even professional money managers can't be sure whether the market is over- or undervalued, it is unrealistic to think that the typical investor can figure it out. Nonetheless, I believe there are three simple strategies that can keep investors grounded—by keeping them focused on the market's fundamental value.

First, we should think like shoppers. When the department store holds a sale, we rush to buy the new jeans that we need. True, there may be an even better sale in three months. But we are happy to buy now, because prices are cheaper than they were. Shouldn't the same thinking apply to the stock market?

To be fair, the analogy doesn't quite work. The jeans we buy on sale today are the same ones that were on the rack yesterday priced at 50 percent more. By contrast, the stocks on sale today are cheaper because investors fear that the fundamental value of corporations has deteriorated, perhaps because the economy is slowing and hence corporate earnings growth may be more sluggish than expected. Still, while share prices can easily fall 10 percent in a week, it's inconceivable that the fundamental value of the underlying corporations would decline that quickly. Changes in the real economy simply don't happen that fast.

Why does a company's share price change faster than its underlying value? Blame it on the short-term outlook of the professional money managers, securities analysts and market strategists who drive the market's day-to-day performance. They are anticipating the future. But the future they care about lies perhaps 12 months ahead, because that's the time period over which their investment performance will be judged and on which their compensation will be based.

Most ordinary investors have time horizons that are far longer than 12 months. When we get a broad market decline and there's a whiff of panic in the air, it's reasonable to assume that tumbling prices reflect worries about the short-term economic outlook—and they don't reflect the strong likelihood that the crisis will prove fleeting and that the long-term outlook is bright. In other words, if all we care about are next year's corporate earnings, maybe the prospect of a recession does justify a 30 percent drop in share prices. But if we are looking out 10 years, the selloff is likely an overreaction, and the rational response is to buy more shares, not sell.

What's the second strategy for keeping ourselves grounded? As we look at the stock market, we might think like bond investors. If we're buying bonds, we are typically more enthusiastic if we receive a yield of 5 percent, rather than 4. Similarly, as we look at stocks, we might think about how much in earnings and dividends we're buying with every $100 invested. That information is widely available for dividends. As of year-end 2015, the companies in the Standard & Poor's 500-stock index were collectively yielding just over 2 percent in annual dividends, or $2 for every $100 invested.

Earnings yields aren't regularly published, but they are easy enough to calculate. Investors often look at a company's price-earnings ratio, or P/E, which is the company's stock price divided by its earnings per share. When you calculate an earnings yield, you simply reverse the calculation, so you divide the earnings by the stock price. If, say, the stocks in the Standard & Poor's 500-index are trading at 20 times earnings, they have an earnings yield of 5 percent. To calculate that 5 percent, you don't need to know the earnings per share for the S&P 500 companies. Instead, there's a shortcut method: You simply divide 100 by the market's price-earnings ratio, which is 20 in this example.[55]

What if stocks subsequently tumble 15 percent? If we focus just on the price decline, we might be unnerved. To stave off panic, we should instead think about the market's earnings and dividend yield. As prices fall, every $100 invested not only buys us more in dividends, but also more in earnings. If the market's price-earnings ratio had been 20 and stock prices fall by 15 percent, the P/E would drop to 17. If we divide 100 by 17, we find the earnings yield is now 6 percent, rather than 5. Like a bond investor who can now buy at higher yields, we should be more enthusiastic about stocks, not less, because every $100 invested is buying us $6 in corporate earnings, rather than $5.

Keep in mind that, unlike the interest from conventional bonds, dividends and earnings aren't fixed. If the economy slows, dividends and especially corporate profits may fall in the short-term, which could potentially make valuations appear less attractive. One solution: Focus less on trailing 12-month reported earnings and more on inflation-adjusted earnings for the past 10 years. The latter is the denominator used in the so-called Shiller P/E, named after Yale University economist Robert Shiller. To learn more, including the current Shiller P/E ratio, check out Robert Shiller's homepage.[56]

While earnings and dividends may slip in the short-term, they should grow over time. If we had invested $100 in the Standard & Poor's 500 at year-end 1995, our dividend yield would have been 2.2 percent and our earnings yield 5.5 percent. Two decades later, the dividend yield on our initial $100 investment would have grown to 7.1 percent and the earnings yield to 14.1 percent. This assumes we spent the dividends we received. If we had reinvested those dividends in additional shares, the earnings and dividend yield on our initial $100 investment would have been even larger.

That brings us to the third strategy for keeping ourselves grounded: We should focus on the market's likely long-run performance. In chapter 2, we talked about the distinction between the stock market's "investment" return and its "speculative" return. The speculative return is driven by changes in the market's P/E, and there's no way to guess what that will be. But over the long haul, it likely won't matter much. Instead, what will drive our stock portfolios' performance is the investment return, comprised of the dividend yield plus earnings growth. In chapter 2, I suggested the long-run investment return might be 6 percent a year, while inflation runs at 2 percent.

As we think about the stock market's future return, we might imagine a line rising steadily at 6 percent every year. The market's actual return will be far more erratic. Sometimes, it will be above this 6 percent-a-year growth line and sometimes below, as other investors are excited one moment and pessimistic the next. If we enjoy great results over a 12-month stretch, we have effectively borrowed from the future, and there's a decent chance we will eventually pay a price, in the form of lower short-run returns. Conversely, when market performance is wretched, we will fall below the 6 percent annual growth path, and—fingers crossed—we should eventually do some catching up. Folks on Wall Street sometimes refer to this as "mean reversion."

Is 6 percent the right number? How long will we have to wait for stocks to revert to their average return? Nobody knows. Still, even with these open questions, there's a notion here that can keep us sane at times of market turmoil. What drives stock returns over the long run are dividend yields and earnings growth. That is what we should focus on. It's just a question of hanging tough until the market recognizes the value that has been created.

THINK (REALLY, REALLY) BIG

We Need to Bring Order to Our Financial Life—By Focusing on Our Paycheck

B rokerage firms want us to trade. Property-casualty insurers want us to take out a big, fat homeowner's policy. Mutual-fund companies push us to open an individual retirement account. Auto dealerships want us to lease a car. Real estate agents prod us to buy a larger home. Credit-card companies hope we use plastic for every purchase. Banks want us to take out a mortgage. Life insurers tout the virtues of cash-value life insurance.

As these companies and their salespeople compete for our business, our financial life is sold to us piecemeal—and we happily embrace this approach, because it appeals to our mental accounting. We like having our finances divvied up into neat little categories, as if they were manila folders in a filing cabinet. Bank statements are in one folder. Insurance is in another. We also have folders for the house, brokerage account, car loan, retirement accounts, credit cards, college accounts and more. The problem: Almost nobody talks about how all these pieces fit together, so we end up with a world overflowing with irrationality. Consider a fistful of examples:

- Young parents will buy auto policies with low $250 deductibles—but not bother with life insurance. These couples are taking minimal risk with their minivan and massive risk if they go under the next bus.

- Folks will carry credit-card balances costing 20 percent—while parking cash in a savings account earning 0.1 percent. Using the savings account to pay down the credit cards is an obvious win. What if these families suddenly need cash? They can always borrow on their credit cards again.

- Employees will work for 30 years at a job they hate to qualify for a traditional defined benefit pension—but they wouldn't dream of delaying Social Security benefits by a few years to get a larger monthly check. We see the same phenomenon with immediate fixed annuities. Many retirees would love to have a traditional pension plan—and yet they balk at using their savings to buy an immediate fixed annuity that pays lifetime income, which would give them a comparable stream of income.

- Couples will buy lottery tickets and take vacations in Vegas—even as they steer clear of stocks because they are afraid of losing money. This is even more irrational than it seems. With lottery tickets and casino gambling, the odds suggest that we will almost certainly lose if we play for long enough. By contrast, time favors a diversified portfolio of stocks, which should deliver handsome gains if we invest for a decade or longer.

- People will load up on canned goods whenever there's a two-for-one special at the grocery store—while failing to stash enough in their employer's retirement plan to get the company's full dollar-for-dollar matching contribution. Both strategies can effectively double our money. Both can put food in our mouths. But only the 401(k) will allow us to spend our retirement eating in restaurants.

- Folks will run screaming with excitement to the shopping mall whenever there's a 50 percent off sale—but they will run screaming with terror from the stock market whenever there's a 50 percent off sale. I discussed the shopping analogy at the end of the last chapter and conceded there was a subtle difference. Still, it highlights our often addled response to market turmoil.

How can we avoid all this irrationality and get a clearer view of this sprawling, messy thing we call a financial life? We should start with what is often our most valuable asset: our income-earning ability or, as economists have dubbed it, our human capital. It's a notion that has long fascinated the dismal science.

In *The Wealth of Nations*, published in 1776, Adam Smith counted the "acquired and useful abilities of all the inhabitants" among a nation's fixed capital. "The most valuable of all capital is that invested in human beings," wrote Alfred Marshall in his 1890 opus *Principles of Economics*. The late Gary S. Becker, a winner of the Nobel Memorial Prize in Economic Sciences, analyzed the financial rate of return from achieving different levels of education. A recent study found that college graduates had expected lifetime earnings that were some 70 percent higher than those who only graduated high school. Another Nobel Prize winner, Robert C. Merton, as well as economists such as Zvi Bodie, Roger Ibbotson and Moshe Milevsky, have discussed our human capital's implications for our financial life, including what combination of stocks and bonds we should hold and which insurance policies we should buy.[57]

For those age 50 or older who have done a decent job of saving and investing, their most valuable asset will probably be their investment portfolio. But for anybody who is younger, the value of their human capital will likely dwarf any other asset they own. Over a 40-year career, our human capital might provide us with earnings of more than $2 million, figured in today's dollars, and perhaps much, much more. We should take this enormously valuable stream of income and design our financial life around it.

That approach has three key advantages, which are discussed in the pages ahead. First, by thinking about our likely lifetime income and the constraints it imposes, we can get a better handle on the financial tradeoffs we need to make. Second, by focusing on the income from our human capital—or the lack thereof—we can build more sensible investment portfolios, with our stock-bond mix designed to complement our human capital's relatively predictable income. Third, by using our paycheck as an organizing principle, we can bring greater rationality to our broader financial life, including which insurance policies to buy and how to handle our debts.

TRADING OFF

Most of us have a laundry list of financial dreams, including a beautiful home, fancy cars, a vacation cottage and college for the kids. But we can't afford to do it all. What should take priority? It's no contest. Chronologically, retirement might be our final financial goal, but we should always put it first.

Amassing enough for a comfortable retirement is our life's great financial task: During our working years, we need to take the income from our human capital and use it to amass a heaping pile of financial capital, so that one day we can live without the income from our human capital. To achieve this goal, we might need to save 10 to 15 percent of our pretax income every year for 30 or 40 years.

Yet retirement often gets short shrift, in large part because we are so focused on immediate goals and so bad at planning for the distant future. We might strive to buy a home in our 30s. In our 40s, our focus often switches to the kids' college education. With those two goals behind us, we finally turn our attention to retirement. But at that point, we might be in our 50s— and it is too late, because 10 or 15 years simply isn't enough time to accumulate the money needed for a comfortable retirement. To avoid shortchanging our retirement and to get maximum advantage from long-term investment compounding, we need to deal with our goals concurrently, rather than consecutively. In other words, even as we tackle more immediate goals, we should also save and invest for retirement.

Financial advisors will sometimes create net worth statements for their clients. They add up the value of a client's assets and then subtract his or her liabilities. The resulting number is the client's net worth. The assets typically consist of the client's investments and perhaps his or her home, while the liabilities might include a mortgage, auto loans, credit-card balances, student loans and other debts. Arguably, however, the definition of assets and liabilities ought to be expanded. The list of assets should include future Social Security benefits, any traditional employer pension and our human capital, while the liabilities should encompass not just our debts, but also the cost of our various goals.

How much will our goals cost? In early 2016, existing homes in the U.S. sold on average for a little over $200,000, according to the National Association of Realtors. Four years at college might run anywhere from $80,000 to $260,000, depending on whether it's a state university or an elite private college. Such sums might seem large—but they pale next to the cost of even a modest retirement.

Let's say we set our sights on a $60,000-a-year retirement. We figure we will receive $20,000 a year from Social Security. For the other $40,000, we would need a $1 million nest egg, assuming we draw down the portfolio using a 4 percent withdrawal rate.[58] Among financial goals, retirement isn't notable just for the fancy price tag. It is also unique in two other respects: It isn't optional and we can't pay for it out of current income.

Families are regularly exhorted to set aside money

for their children's college education. Some savings are also required when buying a home, because we will need to pay closing costs and we will likely have to make at least a modest down payment. But in the end, whether it's a college education or a house, much of the cost is usually paid out of current income. We take out a mortgage and then effectively buy the house on the 30-year installment purchase plan. Moreover, the monthly mortgage payment often isn't much greater than the monthly cost to rent, so there isn't a huge added out-of-pocket cost when we go from renter to homeowner. Similarly, while families might amass some savings to pay for college, they often cover much of the cost out of current income, whether it's paying the bills as they arise or borrowing money and then repaying the loans over time. On top of that, depending on their income and assets, families might receive financial aid to help cover college costs.

By contrast, we can't pay for retirement with our regular paycheck—because at that point we probably won't have one. Don't get me wrong: If it is possible and it's what you want, I am all in favor of staying in the workforce beyond age 65. In fact, there's evidence it can increase longevity.[59] I think working longer will become increasingly common and, for those with skimpy nest eggs, probably a necessity. This should not be a cause for despair. Working at least part-time can bring a sense of purpose to our retirement years and ease the financial strain. If we can earn $16,000 a year by working a few days each week, that's like having a nest egg that is $400,000 larger, based on a 4 percent portfolio withdrawal rate.

Those inclined to nitpick might argue that, if we are working in retirement, we aren't truly retired. But this highlights the craziness of how we think about retirement: To reach this blessed state, apparently we shouldn't dream of doing anything that others might consider productive and for which they would be willing to pay. As mentioned in chapter 2, I hope the distinction between work and retirement gets a whole lot murkier.

My contention: Retirement should be redefined, so it is viewed not as a chance to relax after four exhausting decades, but rather as an opportunity to take on new challenges, without worrying so much about whether those challenges come with a paycheck. We might even take a phased approach to retirement. As our wealth grows, we could use the resulting financial freedom to focus less on pulling in a big paycheck and more on doing work we find fulfilling. That might mean switching to a less lucrative career in our 40s or 50s, or perhaps working fewer hours so we can devote more time to hobbies we are passionate about. In our 60s, we might take this a step further, working part-time and eventually quitting paid work entirely.

But while a phased retirement could be ideal for many folks, it may not be possible, depending on your job—and it has its limits. That brings us to retirement's other unique feature: It isn't optional. I think everybody should endeavor to become a homeowner and I think it is great if parents can pay their children's college costs. But in the end, we don't have to own a home and we don't have to cough up for our children's college education.

By contrast, at some point, most of us will be compelled to pay for retirement. I have met people who hope to keep working until the day they die. I find that admirable, but I don't think it is realistic. Maybe our employer will push us into an unwanted retirement. Maybe ill-health will prevent us from working. Maybe one day we will wake up and find we simply don't have the energy to go to the office. Unless we die prematurely, there's a high likelihood that one day we will leave paid employment—and, at that juncture, we will need a heap of savings to sustain our standard of living.

My advice: Play around with one of the many online calculators and figure out how much you need to save each year for retirement, assuming a relatively modest rate of return. For instance, you might try the Retirement Planner at Dinkytown.net. For the period both before and during retirement, plug in a 4 percent annual return and 2 percent for inflation. True, that's lower than the 6 percent I have estimated for a globally diversified stock portfolio. But you will likely have part of your portfolio in bonds, you need to make allowances for investment costs and it's best to err on the side of caution.

If you discover you are saving enough for retirement, what should you do with the rest of the income from your human capital? That's your call. You might opt for the bigger home, the flashier car, the vacation cottage or the ritzy private college for the kids. But you shouldn't set your heart on any of these goals until you are confident that you're on track for a financially comfortable retirement.

BONDING WITH OURSELVES

If someone mentioned a way to get steady income for 40 years, most investors would immediately think, "Ah, we're talking about a bond." That, in a nutshell, is how we should think about our paycheck. To be sure, there are important differences between our human capital and a bond. With any luck, we will receive salary increases during our career, while bond investors usually don't enjoy rising income. If our luck isn't so good, we might miss a few paychecks because we occasionally lose our job and can't quickly find a new employer. Another difference: While investors receive a bond's principal value when the bond matures, our human capital doesn't have any principal value.

Still, the similarities are greater than the differences—and our human capital's bond-like income should influence how we invest. When we are in our 20s, with 40 years of paychecks ahead of us, we effectively have a huge position in bonds. We don't need regular income from our portfolio, because we have a paycheck to cover our living costs. That frees us up to invest heavily in stocks, with the goal of earning healthy, inflation-beating gains. Those gains could make accumulating our target nest egg far easier. What if the stock market crashes? During our time in the workforce, a market plunge might be unnerving. But it shouldn't have any impact on our standard of living. We have the income from our human capital, so there's no need to sell stocks to buy groceries.

A market decline probably also wouldn't have much impact on our overall net worth. Suppose we suffered a repeat of the 2007–09 market collapse, with its 57 percent plunge by the Standard & Poor's 500-stock index. That would devastate our stock portfolio's value, but it might barely dent the value of our total assets. In addition to our human capital, our assets might include our home, a traditional employer pension plan, the money we have in bonds and cash investments, and our future Social Security benefit. The market's collapse—with its emotional impact magnified by cable business channels and frightening newspaper headlines—might make us fearful for our financial future. But the reality is, we are so much more than the sum of our stocks and our stock funds.

Once we retire and our paycheck disappears, all this changes. Our human capital "bond" no longer pays us regular income, so it's hard to be sanguine about plunging financial markets. A stock market crash could have a devastating impact on our ability to pay the bills. That's why, as we approach retirement, we should shift perhaps half of our portfolio out of stocks and into bonds. As we consider precisely how much to allocate to bonds, we should factor in three other streams of bond-like income: our Social Security benefit, any traditional employer pension plan and any income annuity we have purchased. If these will cover a substantial portion of our monthly retirement costs, we might risk keeping somewhat more of our portfolio in stocks.

The shift toward bonds has two benefits. First, bonds typically kick off more income than stocks, so we will have more investment income to replace the lost income from our human capital. Second, and more important, we will have a buffer against stock market turmoil. Once retired, to generate enough spending money, we will likely need to sell a sliver of our portfolio's holdings every so often, to supplement whatever we receive from investment income, Social Security, any traditional employer pension and any income annuities. What if we get hit with a vicious stock-market decline? If we have a balanced investment mix, there should be no need to panic, because we can always generate spending money by selling from the bond side of our portfolio.

While this lifecycle approach to portfolio building will make sense for most folks, keep two caveats in mind. First, during their working years, some people's earnings will be more bond-like than others. If you are a tenured professor, you have a pretty good idea of how big your paycheck will be a year from now. If you are a salesperson who works on commission, there's far less certainty. The implication: Tenured professors could invest heavily in stocks, assuming they have the stomach for it, while those who work on commission might include a bigger dollop of bonds.

Second, because our human capital accounts for such a large portion of our total wealth, we should be careful not to double down on that bet. That means that Silicon Valley employees should think twice before buying technology stocks. Doctors shouldn't invest in pharmaceutical and medical device companies. Real estate agents should avoid real estate investment trusts and rental properties. And all of us should keep holdings of our employer's stock to a bare minimum.

We might feel comfortable with these investments because they are familiar, and we might even feel like our jobs give us added investment insight. The reality: Even if a company is thriving, it doesn't mean its stock is a good investment. The odds are, other investors have also noticed that the company is prospering—and its heady prospects may be fully reflected in the company's heady stock market valuation. More important, our sense of comfort and our belief that we have some special insight can blind us to a huge risk: If we invest heavily in our employer's stock and the company gets into financial trouble, we could suffer a double whammy, losing both our job and a big chunk of our nest egg.

All this talk of human capital and how to divvy up a portfolio might have some readers scratching their heads. Don't we invest heavily in stocks in our 20s because we have decades to ride out market downturns? This notion of "time diversification" is fiercely debated in academic circles. If market returns are random, there is no guarantee that stocks will beat bonds, no matter how long we hang on. In fact, as we lengthen our time horizon, we could end up with far more or far less wealth than we imagined, as the effect of good and bad years are magnified through the process of investment compounding. For instance, I think it's reasonable to expect annual stock market returns averaging 6 percent, which would translate to a 929 percent cumulative gain over 40 years. But if just three of those 40 years turn out to be 25 percent losses rather than 6 percent gains, the cumulative return would be 264 percent, equal to a mere 3.3 percent a year.[60]

This might sound unnerving, but it's less of a problem than it seems. Most of us don't make a single stock-market purchase when we enter the workforce, and then cross our fingers and hope the market is kind for the next four decades. Instead, we make small monthly purchases over those 40 years. Yes, we will likely accumulate more wealth if the stock market generates a higher cumulative return over those four decades. But the range of possible outcomes probably won't be as wide as the example in the preceding paragraph suggests, because our monthly purchases will buy stocks at all kinds of different prices, some high, some low. Moreover, a stretch of rotten market returns might work to our benefit, because it would allow us to buy shares at cheaper prices.

On top of that, the debate over time diversification hinges on the assumption that market movements are random. That seems reasonable if we are looking at short-term results. But over the long term, commonsense suggests that—in the absence of an economic apocalypse—markets ought to be mean reverting. If we have a string of lousy years for the stock market, presumably stocks would become better and better value, as share prices tumble faster than dividends and earnings. Those dividends and earnings may slip in the short term, but they should eventually resume growing. At some point, bargain-hunting investors would notice and their buying would drive share prices back up.

LENDING A HAND

Why is it considered okay for college students to take on $30,000 or $40,000 in education loans? Why do so many employers provide disability insurance? Why are banks happy to lend $500,000 to 28-year-olds purchasing their first home? Why are couples who are starting a family encouraged to buy life insurance? Once again, it's all about our human capital.

When the federal government lends money to students, or banks lend money to young homebuyers, they know that most borrowers will be able to repay the loans, because the borrowers have many decades of paychecks ahead of them. This is a deal where both sides benefit: The lenders collect interest, while the borrowers can buy items they couldn't otherwise afford. If we had to pay cash for every purchase, many of us would struggle to afford college, and we might not be able to buy our first home until our 40s or 50s. Borrowing allows us to smooth out consumption over our lifetime, by making it possible to buy items before we have saved up the full purchase price. This is a huge plus. By borrowing so we can pay for college, we increase our likely lifetime earnings. By buying a home in our 20s or 30s, we can build up home equity and come to own a major asset free and clear.

That said, we should be careful not to overdo this consumption smoothing. If we borrow to buy luxury cars in our 20s, we won't get the lifetime pleasure that comes with a gradually rising standard of living. It's better to buy the Honda in our 20s, so the Lexus we own in our 50s seems more special.

We also need to be careful not to borrow too much. The size of our mortgage, and the amount of student debt we take on, should be guided by our likely earnings. According to the so-called debt ratio that is used by many banks, those with mortgages should limit their total monthly debt payments to 36 percent of pretax income. That means someone earning $5,000 a month shouldn't be putting more than $1,800 toward car loans, minimum credit-card payments, student loans and mortgage payments, including property taxes and homeowner's insurance. What if you don't have a mortgage—and instead you're trying to figure out what's a prudent amount to borrow for college costs? I would think about your likely annual earnings in the decade after graduation, and try to limit your debts so that the resulting loan payments are 10 percent or less of your expected income. To avoid breaching that threshold, those with lower expected earnings may need to favor less costly colleges.

Even as we limit the amount of income devoted to debt servicing, we should also aim to have all debts paid off before we collect our last paycheck and quit the workforce. If, say, we trade up to a larger home in our 40s, we should seriously consider taking out a 15-year or 20-year mortgage, so the loan is paid off before we retire. What if we opt for a 30-year mortgage instead, perhaps because we don't want to lock ourselves into such high monthly payments? We might make extra-principal payments, with the goal of ridding ourselves of the mortgage by the time we retire. That will lower our cost of living and make retirement more affordable.

Paying down debt is, in any case, often a smart investment. We should think of our debts as negative bonds. When we buy bonds, we lend money to others and, in return, they pay us interest. When we borrow money, the roles are reversed: Others lend to us and we pay them interest. Because we are considered less creditworthy than the federal government and major corporations, we typically have to pay a higher interest rate on our debts than we can earn by buying their bonds. An obvious conclusion: Instead of purchasing bonds, certificates of deposit and other interest-generating investments, it often makes sense to pay down debt.

By thinking of our debts as negative bonds, we can also get a better handle on our family's overall financial risk. Imagine a brother and sister, both with $500,000 portfolios. The brother has $300,000 in stocks and $200,000 in bonds, while the sister's $500,000 is invested entirely in the stock market. Based purely on their portfolios, it might appear that the sister's financial situation is riskier. But what if the sister has no debt, while the brother has a $200,000 mortgage? If we subtract his $200,000 mortgage from his $200,000 in bonds, the brother's net bond position is effectively zero, so his finances are arguably just as risky as his sister's and perhaps more so, depending on their relative net worth, job situation, financial obligations and other factors.

Suppose the brother's bonds are sitting in a regular taxable account, and hence he doesn't have to worry about the income taxes and possible tax penalties levied on retirement account withdrawals. He would likely be better off selling his $200,000 in bonds and using the proceeds to pay off his mortgage, because the interest rate he pays on his mortgage is probably higher than the interest rate he is earning on his bonds. Yes, to figure out whether this is a smart move, the brother needs to take into account the tax deductibility of his mortgage interest—but he should also consider any taxes he pays on the interest from his bonds.

We all engage in mental accounting, associating the mortgage with the house and the car loan with the sedan. But once we have these debts, they effectively leverage our entire financial life. Again, consider the brother's financial situation, with his $500,000 portfolio and $200,000 mortgage. Let's say he had used the mortgage to purchase a $300,000 home. The brother effectively owns an $800,000 collection of real estate, stocks and bonds, a quarter of which was bought with borrowed money, thanks to the $200,000 mortgage. The brother would likely be horrified to learn that he is betting on stocks with borrowed money, and yet that's what he is effectively doing.

Whether the brother is taking too much risk will depend heavily on his human capital. How secure is his job—and how steady is his income? This should influence how much debt he takes on and what type.

If the brother is a government employee, his job is likely pretty secure and his income highly predictable. His human capital doesn't involve much risk, so he can probably take a fair amount of risk in the rest of his financial life, including investing heavily in stocks, taking on debt payments equal to 36 percent of pretax income and perhaps opting for an adjustable-rate mortgage, which may have a relatively low interest rate but will also involve fluctuating monthly payments. Conversely, if the brother is a Wall Street trader, his human capital involves a lot of risk. Traders are often laid off during market downturns, so the brother should probably hold more bonds in his portfolio, keep his debt payments well below 36 percent of income and favor the relative certainty of a fixed-rate mortgage.

Whether the brother is a trader or a government worker, he ought to have health insurance, and he probably needs life and disability insurance. Again, it's all about the risk associated with our human capital. If we are sick and unable to pay for medical help, that will affect our ability to work, so it's crucial to have health insurance.

What about buying disability and life insurance, in case we're unable to provide for our family? Much depends on our net worth and family situation. If we have enough set aside so that we could retire today, we probably don't need disability insurance, because we would be okay financially if an illness or accident prevented us from working. Similarly, if we have enough to retire or nobody depends on us financially, we can likely also do without life insurance. But if we have little in savings, we ought to have disability insurance, and if we have little in savings plus a family that relies on our income-earning ability, we definitely need life insurance. There's more on insurance in the next chapter.

LOOSE ENDS

Our income-earning ability is the thread that can help tie together the many disparate parts of our financial life. But as we try to get a handle on the big financial picture, there are three notions that are only tangentially related to our human capital—and yet I would be remiss in not mentioning them.

First, as we keep tabs on the state of our overall finances, we shouldn't overlook one of the key financial levers at our disposal: our ability to vary our spending. Suppose we are retired and we're concerned because financial markets have fallen sharply. We might be tempted to play around with our investment mix. But often, a smarter response is to stick with our target mix of stocks and bonds, and instead cut our spending. That would reduce the amount we need to withdraw from our portfolio. Maybe it's the year to nix the overseas vacation and take a U.S. road trip instead. Maybe we should keep the old car for another year or two, rather than trading it in for a newer model. Our ability to vary our spending will be greater if we keep our fixed costs low, including the amount we devote each month to mortgage or rent, car payments, utilities, insurance premiums, groceries and other regularly recurring costs.

Second, if we are managing our money for a long life, we should try to ensure our body lasts almost as long. Let's say we smoke, drink heavily and never exercise. In all likelihood, we will shorten our life expectancy and hence the amount we need for retirement. Call me crazy, but if folks are smoking two packs a day while also maxing out their 401(k), they probably aren't being entirely rational.

Finally, as we think about our assets and liabilities, we shouldn't overlook our parents, spouse and children. Family can be an invaluable asset: If we are in financial difficulty, they may ride to our rescue. A supportive family might mean we can hold a smaller emergency fund and carry higher deductibles on our various insurance policies.

But family can also be a liability. We should think long and hard before getting married—and even longer and harder before getting divorced, because it's a great way to lose half our wealth. What if our parents or children get into financial trouble? We shouldn't kid ourselves: We will almost certainly bail them out. This is why we should talk to our elderly parents about their finances and why we should make every effort to raise financially responsible children.

As I suggested in chapter 3, good savings habits are the key to financial success. If there's any financial skill we should endeavor to teach our children, it's the ability to delay gratification. This isn't just about encouraging our kids to save up their pocket money for larger purchases. When we tell our children that they can't play until after they have practiced piano, or they can't have candy until after they have had lunch, we are teaching them to delay gratification. Regularly discussing financial issues can also help. But more important is the example we set and the family stories we tell. We should talk to our children about how we scrimped and saved in our 20s, so they will be prepared to scrimp and save when they get into the workforce.

Every so often, when I was at *The Wall Street Journal*, I would receive emails from readers, boasting about how they had managed to retire in their 40s. I would immediately write back, asking a single question, "Do you have children?" The answer was almost always "no." Make no mistake: People who have kids retire later. This book is dedicated to my two children and two stepchildren. Two of the four kids are off the family payroll. Two remain partially funded liabilities. All four have enriched my life. My bank account? Not so much.

STEP NO. 5:

TO WIN, DON'T LOSE

If We Want to Add to Our Wealth, We Should Minimize the Subtractions

W hat is financial success? Some of us might get a warm glow from amassing more money than our brother-in-law, beating the Standard & Poor's 500-stock index or having the best toys in the neighborhood. But those are just bragging rights that can slip away as quickly as they're acquired. The goal isn't to get rich.

Rather, the goal is to have enough money to lead the life we want. The life I desire is no doubt different from the one you would choose. But our wish lists likely have a few common themes: We want time with friends and family. We want special moments like dinners out and vacations. We want to devote our days to activities we're passionate about. And we want these things without constantly worrying about money.

If this sort of financial freedom is the overriding goal, it becomes more obvious what our financial choices should be. Unless we're banking on reincarnation, we have just one shot at making the journey from birth to retirement, so flirting with financial failure is not advisable. Instead, we should pursue strategies that have a high likelihood of success and, once we have amassed enough money to pay for the life we want, we should be careful to remain winners, rather than taking unnecessary risks that could snatch defeat from the jaws of victory.

Back in chapter 3, I mentioned wagering on a coin flip. If we call heads or tails correctly, we win $100, while getting it wrong would cost us $100. It is a fair bet—and yet one that we shy away from. To persuade us to risk $100 on a coin flip, the prize for calling heads or tails correctly would likely need to be $200 and perhaps more. This suggests we get far more pain from losses than pleasure from gains. Economists consider this irrational.

Perhaps we are too loss averse. But arguably, we should be at least somewhat averse to losses. If we regularly make investment bets where there's a 50-50 chance of success or failure, and luck is on our side, we could end up rich, which is appealing. But if we make such bets and we aren't so lucky, we might never have enough money for retirement, which would be an unmitigated disaster. Even if the risk of making or losing money is equal, the consequences are not.

Don't misunderstand me: I'm not advocating that investors shy away from all risk by, say, stuffing their savings in bank accounts and certificates of deposit backed by the FDIC. CDs may save us from short-term losses, but they will leave us vulnerable to inflation and they might not generate sufficient gains to pay for a comfortable retirement. To amass the wealth we need to lead the life we want, most of us should own at least some stocks. But even as we strive to increase our net worth, we should also focus on minimizing subtractions. What subtractions? We're talking here about fending off not only high costs that eat away at our wealth, but also major threats that could derail our financial future. Minimizing these subtractions will likely be a far more productive use of our time than pursuing extra gains.

Often, as we contemplate making a change to our investment mix, we will ask ourselves a question like, "Is this a good time to buy stocks?" But this is the wrong question to ask, because we find ourselves answering based on something that is unknowable, which is the market's short-term direction. Instead, we should reframe the issue, and ask instead about risk and investment costs. "How much will it cost, in investment expenses and taxes, to make this portfolio change? Is that a reasonable amount to pay given the possible—but far from certain—benefit? How will it affect my overall portfolio's risk level? If I make this investment bet and I am wrong, can I live with the financial impact?"

We can't control whether the markets go up or down, and there's no surefire strategy for outperforming the market averages. But that doesn't mean all is uncertain with our portfolio and with our broader financial life. While we may not have a crystal ball, we still have three great financial levers at our disposal. As discussed in earlier chapters, we can control how much we spend and save, and that's typically the biggest driver of our financial success.

But we shouldn't overlook the two other levers. We can control how much we incur in financial costs, including money management fees, trading costs, taxes, insurance premiums and more. And we can control the financial risks we are exposed to, by being prudent in how we build our portfolios and being smart about the insurance we buy.

LOSING SLOWLY

There are two ways that wealth dies: It can die slowly and it can die quickly. Let's start with the slow death—what I think of as the death by a thousand cuts. A classic example is the almost silent subtraction from our wealth caused by investment costs and taxes.

Suppose that, for 40 years, we stashed money on a regular basis in a broad stock market index fund. Vanguard Group founder John C. Bogle calculates that we would accumulate 65 percent more wealth than an investor who owns an actively managed stock fund, with its higher trading costs, higher management fees and larger cash holdings. Those cash holdings might reflect a fund manager's bearishness or a dearth of good stock-picking ideas, while also providing money to meet shareholder redemptions.

All told, Bogle calculates that the total annual cost of investing in an actively managed stock fund might amount to 2.27 percent a year, equal to $2.27 for every $100 invested. By contrast, owning an index fund that tracks the broad U.S. stock market could cost just 0.06 percent a year, or 6 cents per $100 invested.[61] The difference in total cost between bond index funds and actively managed bond funds is somewhat less, but the result is still the same: Those who index are likely to amass far more wealth over the long run.

Paying 2 percent or so every year for an actively managed stock fund might not sound so bad, especially when set against the prospect of market-beating gains. But those market-beating gains are likely to prove elusive, partly because of the drag from investment costs and partly because it's so hard for active managers to uncover undervalued stocks. Moreover, the cost of active management isn't nearly as modest as it appears. Yes, we might pay 2 percent of assets per year, which doesn't seem like a huge sum when it's framed that way. But in a world where stocks could return just 6 percent a year, we are surrendering a staggering 33 percent of our potential gain to investment costs.

Bogle's 65 percent wealth gap is for a retirement account investor, and hence this figure ignores the impact of taxes. Actively managed stock funds tend to generate significantly larger annual tax bills than index funds, as managers sell one stock and buy another, in an effort to score market-beating gains. That trading can cause actively managed funds to realize large capital gains each year, on which taxable shareholders then have to pay taxes. Meanwhile, most index funds generate little or no realized capital gains, because they don't actively trade their portfolios. Bogle figures that if an investor made a onetime investment in an index fund and then held on for 40 years, the investor would accumulate 175 percent more wealth, after factoring in taxes, than an investor who owned an actively managed fund.

All this can be made worse by the behavior of

investors themselves. It isn't simply that investors might trade in and out of the stock market at the wrong time. To add salt to that potential wound, all this trading can trigger big tax bills. Even if investors own index funds, which should generate modest annual tax bills, they can inflict large tax bills on themselves by rapidly trading their fund holdings and thereby realizing capital gains.

This is not to suggest that fund investors behave less sensibly than those who hold individual company shares. There's ample evidence that ordinary investors don't do themselves any favors when dabbling in individual stocks.[62] There are also plenty of other ways that we inflict the slow financial death upon ourselves. We get our mortgage from the local bank, rather than scouring the Internet for the lender offering the lowest mortgage rate and lowest fees. We shortchange ourselves by carrying a credit-card balance and paying the exorbitant finance charges. We fail to put enough in our 401(k) to earn the full matching employer contribution. We don't shop around for a higher yield when opening a savings account or buying a certificate of deposit. We purchase our new auto policy from our existing insurer, rather than getting quotes from a variety of companies. We repeatedly overdraw our bank account with debit-card charges, getting dinged $35 every time.

Nonetheless, the example of index funds vs. actively managed stock funds is instructive, because it raises the specter not only of costs, but also of risk. Imagine we are trying to settle on an investment strategy. We could simply buy and hold a collection of low-cost index funds that gives us worldwide exposure to stocks and bonds. This is an obvious starting point:

We are buying a global collection of investments, with the amount invested in each stock and bond and in each country reflecting their market weighting, so we are essentially piggybacking on the collective wisdom of millions of other investors. They have done the hard work of trying to figure out what stocks and bonds are worth, and then cast their vote with each buy and sell that they make. By indexing, we benefit from their hard work without incurring any of the costs involved.

In our delusional self-confidence, however, we might decide that we are smarter than the collective judgment of all other investors, so we deviate from a global indexing strategy. Depending on how much we deviate, we may put ourselves on course for the slow financial death, because we pay so much more in investment costs and taxes. History tells us that we are highly unlikely to pick investments that outpace the market by a large enough margin to overcome the costs we incur. Chapter 3 spelled out the brutal logic behind this failure: Before costs, investors collectively earn the market's return. After costs, they must inevitably earn less. Some people may get lucky and beat the market, but most won't.

There is, however, a related and perhaps more worrisome issue. As we stray from an indexing strategy, we don't just rack up greater investment costs. We also increase the risk that our investment results will fall far behind the market—and the further we stray from a portfolio that looks like the broad market, the greater the danger of spectacularly bad performance. In Wall Street speak, this is called "tracking error," an obfuscation that makes a potentially major financial loss sound like a minor mishap.

Imagine that we bet our financial future on a fistful

of actively managed funds. Our funds might cost us roughly 2 percentage points a year more than the expenses charged by a low-cost index fund. But while the performance gap between low-cost index funds and the average for all active funds will reflect this difference in expenses, we could be unlucky with the actively managed funds we pick or the market sectors we bet on, and the gap could be far wider than 2 percentage points. What if the gaps get too wide? We are no longer talking about the slow financial death. Instead, we are talking about the quick death—the death by Russian roulette.

DYING QUICKLY

Russian roulette is a game that involves putting a single bullet in a revolver, spinning the cylinder, pointing the gun at your temple and pulling the trigger. If there are six chambers and five are empty, most of the time you will live. But while the odds favor survival, no sane person would consider it a low-risk game. What is the financial equivalent? We are talking about leaving ourselves exposed to potential disasters that could devastate our finances. Here are just some of the nightmare scenarios:

- We become disabled and can't work, we don't have much in savings—and yet we never bothered to buy disability insurance. Can't imagine doing anything so dangerous that you would suffer a disability? Keep in mind that the vast majority of disabilities are caused by illness, not accidents.

- We load up on our employer's stock in our 401(k) plan—and our employer turns out to be the next AIG, Bear Stearns, Enron, Lehman Brothers or

WorldCom, all major companies that suffered spectacular collapses in the last 15 years.

- Our spouse, who is the family's main breadwinner, dies suddenly. We have neither life insurance to collect on nor much in savings—but we do have three children and a hefty mortgage.

- A booming stock market boosts our self-confidence, we load up on stocks, we get a repeat of 2007–09's 57 percent decline—and we panic and sell when our stocks are worth half what we paid.

- We pour our savings into a few rental properties, we have trouble finding tenants, we can't make the mortgage payments—and we wind up in foreclosure.

- We don't have health insurance—and we get diagnosed with cancer.

- We bet everything on one country's stock market—and that country turns out to be the next Japan. At year-end 1989, the Nikkei 225 hit its all-time high. More than a quarter century later, Japanese stocks remain stalled at less than half their 1989 level. Can't see that happening here in the U.S.? In 1989, no economy was more admired than Japan's, and ambitious American businessmen and women were regularly exhorted to learn Japanese.

The problem with the above strategies is that we can roll along for years, completely oblivious to the risks we are taking and maybe even thinking that we are pretty darn clever. And then one day—bam!—we are set back financially by 10 or 20 years. That brings us to the 17th century philosopher and mathematician, Blaise Pascal, and what's come to be known as Pascal's wager. As Pascal saw it, it was rational to believe in God. If we believed and it turned out there was no God, the price was modest: an hour every Sunday on our knees and perhaps a little less immorality. But if we didn't believe and it turned out God did indeed exist, the price was somewhat higher: an eternity burning in hell.[63]

In other words, we should focus less on the odds of success or failure, and more on the consequences. Maybe we can get through life successfully with no health and disability insurance. Maybe we will be okay with a handful of hot stocks or a few heavily mortgaged rental properties. Maybe we will win again and again at Russian roulette. But all it takes is one loss, and our happy financial future will die a quick death.

How can we avoid the quick financial death? It's all about managing risk, and that means buying the right insurance and making sure we invest prudently.

SHARING RISK

With some frequency, financial planners have told me that they have clients who refuse to get a will, because they think it somehow puts them closer to death. This same ignore-it-and-hope-it-never-happens attitude often comes into play with insurance. Most folks buy homeowner's insurance because their mortgage company insists and they purchase auto insurance because their state requires it. Similarly, if families don't have health insurance through their employer, many will now buy it because—if they don't—they face penalties under federal law.

But nobody forces us to buy life, disability,

umbrella-liability and long-term-care insurance, and many Americans don't bother, either because they don't think about it—or because they don't want to think about it. But maybe it's time to ponder the unpleasant: How would our families cope if we died tomorrow, became disabled, got sued or needed nursing home care? We might skip umbrella-liability insurance because we have few assets and thus we figure we aren't worth suing. Similarly, we might not bother with long-term-care insurance because we don't have much in savings, and hence we are happy to spend down what little money we have and then rely on Medicaid. But for many folks, lawsuits and nursing home costs will loom large, and purchasing insurance could make sense.

Even more of us will conclude that we need life and disability insurance. Some people get disability coverage through their employer, and possibly also a limited amount of life insurance. But those who are self-employed, or who don't have employer coverage, should seriously consider disability insurance, especially if they have little in savings and thus their financial life would quickly unravel if they couldn't work. Life insurance also makes sense for those who have families who depend on them financially, but who don't have substantial savings.

All of these disaster scenarios—becoming disabled, paying nursing home costs, getting sued, the main family breadwinner's dying—could wipe out whatever wealth we have and leave us dependent on the government or on the kindness of others. None is particularly fun to contemplate. But failing to think through the unthinkable won't just make our family's financial life more perilous. It can also leave us with a gnawing sense of worry that, with a few simple steps, we could easily extinguish.

This doesn't mean we should buy blanket coverage. Insurance companies typically pay out less to customers than they collect in premiums, so purchasing insurance will usually be a money-losing proposition, plus the cost of all that coverage could blow the family budget. How can we ensure we buy only the insurance that we need? Consider a three-pronged approach.

First, avoid policies that protect against negligible financial risks. It might be upsetting if we need to cancel the flight at the last minute or replace the television we bought last year. But the cost likely wouldn't devastate our finances, so we should usually take a pass on trip-cancellation insurance and extended warranties. Sure, it might be worth buying the warranty on the tablet computer we buy for our eight-year-old, because the tablet won't be handled with care. Yes, it might be worth taking out trip-cancellation insurance if we're age 80, because ill-health could prevent us from travelling. But most of the time, these sorts of insurance policies should be avoided, because the cost is exorbitant relative to the financial risk involved—and that risk is, in any case, minimal.

While we can shoulder some risks on our own, others come with financial consequences that are potentially so grave that we simply have to share the risk with others. This is the notion of risk pooling, which we discussed in chapter 2. We toss dollars into an insurance fund that covers, say, homes burning down and life-insurance payouts, knowing we probably won't get any money back—but also knowing we are covered if disaster strikes.

That brings us to the second strategy: To cut the cost of the insurance we need, we should tweak the coverage, so we assume a modest amount of risk, while leaving the insurance company to handle the bulk of the financial threat. For instance, we might opt for a $4,000 deductible on our homeowner's policy. If the place goes up in flames, we would suffer a $4,000 loss, but the insurer is still on the hook for the big financial hit. Similarly, to lower our premiums, we might opt for higher deductibles on our health and auto policies, and accept a longer elimination period on our disability and long-term-care insurance. The elimination period is the time between when we make our claim and when benefits start getting paid. Until benefits begin, we would have to pay out of pocket, but the cost likely wouldn't break the bank.

Third, we should drop insurance policies as our wealth grows and we are able to shoulder more financial risk. If we have a seven-figure portfolio, our families would likely be okay financially if we died or became disabled, so we might let our life and disability coverage lapse. Similarly, if we have a $1 million nest egg, we could probably eschew long-term-care insurance and instead commit to paying nursing home costs out of pocket, otherwise known as self-insuring. What about umbrella-liability insurance, which can protect us if we find ourselves on the wrong end of a lawsuit? If anything, it becomes increasingly necessary as we grow richer, because we become a more tempting target for the litigious.

FALLING BEHIND

When we invest, we face three distinct risks: There is a risk the markets will generate terrible results, there is a risk our investments will underperform the market averages, and there's a risk that we fare worse still, because we buy and sell these investments at the wrong time.

If every market generates terrible results, we are out of luck. Fortunately, this is unlikely to happen. When inflation accelerates, our bonds will suffer, but the value of our house and our stocks should hold their own, and our salary will likely rise with inflation. When recession threatens, our stocks will slide, home prices may struggle and we could lose our job. But our bonds should fare just fine, and we might also receive help from any alternative investments we own. The alternative investments category includes a hodgepodge of investments, such as gold stocks, timber, hedge funds, natural resources companies and real estate investment trusts. By spreading our investment dollars across a broad array of assets, we buy ourselves some protection against turbulent markets, and we should do reasonably well over the long haul.

What about the performance of our investments relative to the markets? Above, I mentioned using a globally diversified portfolio of index funds as a starting point when deciding what investment mix to hold. Institutional investors and academics sometimes talk about the "market portfolio" or the "investable universe." This is the array of global investments that we can potentially purchase. A 2014 study concluded that the investable universe consisted of 36 percent stocks, 55 percent bonds, 5 percent commercial real estate and 4 percent private equity.[64] The latter involves making venture capital investments in privately held companies. U.S. stocks account for roughly half of the global stock market's value and U.S. bonds account for roughly half of the global bond market.

If we are inclined to avoid all bets and instead piggyback on the collective judgment of others, we could purchase a collection of index funds that replicates this mix.[65] That would give us a portfolio that reflects what all other investors collectively own. This is the ultimate portfolio for those who want average market results before costs—and better-than-average results, relative to other investors, once we factor in the drag from high investment costs on the performance of these other investors.

Still, I am not inclined to fully replicate the global market portfolio, for three key reasons. First, as discussed in chapter 4, our stock-bond mix should reflect our human capital, or lack thereof. The market portfolio has some 55 percent in bonds. Retirees might want to be that conservative, but those still collecting a paycheck should probably have a smaller allocation to bonds.

Second, our portfolio should reflect our personal tolerance for risk. If we're in our 20s with a secure job and a steady paycheck, a 90 percent stock allocation might make sense. But if we are skittish about market gyrations, it wouldn't be smart to own such a volatile investment mix, no matter how young we are.

Third, our holdings should mesh with our future spending. When we retire and start drawing down our nest egg, we will spend most of our savings on U.S. goods and services, so it seems wise to keep the bulk of our portfolio in dollar-denominated investments. Thus, while the U.S. accounts for roughly half of global stock and bond market value, I keep more than 60 percent of my stock portfolio in U.S. stocks and almost

100 percent of my bond market money in U.S. bonds.

MIXING IT UP

What does this mean in practical terms? Let's keep things simple, ignore private equity and commercial real estate, and focus just on the broad stock and bond market. You might buy three funds: an index fund offering exposure to the entire U.S. stock market, an index fund that will give you exposure to both developed foreign stock markets and emerging stock markets, and an index fund that owns the broad U.S. bond market.

Suppose we were aiming to build a classic balanced portfolio, with 60 percent in stocks and 40 percent in bonds. Here are some possible investment mixes using index funds offered by major financial firms:

- 40 percent Fidelity Spartan Total Market Index Fund, 20 percent Fidelity Spartan Global ex U.S. Index Fund and 40 percent Fidelity Spartan U.S. Bond Index Fund. You can purchase these mutual funds directly from Fidelity Investments (Fidelity.com).

- 40 percent Vanguard Total Stock Market Index Fund, 20 percent Vanguard FTSE All-World ex-US Index Fund and 40 percent Vanguard Total Bond Market Index Fund. You can buy these mutual funds directly from Vanguard Group (Vanguard.com).

- 40 percent Vanguard Total Stock Market ETF, 20 percent Vanguard FTSE All-World ex-US ETF and 40 percent Vanguard Total Bond Market ETF. You can purchase these ETFs, or exchange-traded funds, through a discount or full-service brokerage firm. You can learn more about each of the funds at Vanguard.com.

- 40 percent iShares Core S&P Total U.S. Stock Market ETF, 20 percent iShares Core MSCI Total International Stock ETF and 40 percent iShares Core U.S. Aggregate Bond ETF. You can buy these ETFs through a brokerage account and find fund details at iShares.com.

- 40 percent SPDR Russell 3000 ETF, 20 percent SPDR MSCI ACWI ex-US ETF and 40 percent SPDR Barclays Aggregate Bond ETF. You can invest in these ETFs through a brokerage account and learn more at SPDRs.com.

- 40 percent Schwab Total Stock Market Index Fund, 20 percent Schwab International Index Fund and 40 percent Schwab Total Bond Market Fund. You can buy these mutual funds directly from Charles Schwab (Schwab.com). The good news: Schwab's funds have a minimum initial investment of just $100. The bad news: Unlike the other foreign stock funds listed here, Schwab's international index fund focuses solely on developed foreign markets. Those who want exposure to emerging markets might take a fifth of the money allocated to the international fund— equal to 4 percent of the entire portfolio—and invest it in an emerging markets stock index fund. One option: Schwab has an ETF that focuses on emerging markets.

In picking among the funds listed above, pay careful attention to each fund's annual expenses, as well as to the brokerage commission and other trading costs associated with purchasing ETFs. The mutual funds are all no-load funds, meaning there's no commission when you buy or sell. Once you have your portfolio set up, be sure to check back occasionally to make sure your investment mix is still in line with your target portfolio percentages. If it isn't, consider rebalancing, by lightening up on winning investments and adding to those that are below your target percentages. Got a question about index funds or investing in general? You might post it to Bogleheads.org, a great forum for those seeking sensible investment advice.

At this juncture, we have strayed fairly far from the global market portfolio, though solely for reasons of risk and not in a way that would imperil our chances of earning reasonable long-run returns. Should we stray even further? We could second-guess the stocks and bonds held within the index funds—and start actively managing our portfolio. That's not something I am inclined to do. If we shun index funds and instead purchase actively managed funds, there's a risk that the funds we pick will underperform an indexing strategy by a wide margin. That danger grows even larger if we focus our money on a single part of the global stock market or, riskier still, if we start picking individual stocks.

To be sure, by shunning actively managed funds and individual stocks, we also abandon any hope, however slim, of outperforming the indexes. It's the double-edged sword of investing: The less diversified we are, the greater the chance we will get rich—but also the greater the chance we will end up poor. These two outcomes, however, are far from equal.

Remember, the goal is to have enough money to

lead the life we want. We put that at risk if we own a badly diversified portfolio, because we may get hit with huge short-term losses that are extraordinarily hard to recover from. The math of investment losses is daunting: If we lose 25 percent, we need a 33 percent gain to get back to even. Lose 50 percent, and it will take a 100 percent rebound to make us whole. What if we lose 75 percent? To recoup that loss, we would need a 300 percent gain.

A 75 percent loss might seem unthinkable—the sort of improbable nightmare scenario favored by overly cautious financial writers looking to scare their readers. But many U.S. investors have been living this nightmare: Those who bet heavily on technology stocks in the late 1990s suffered even bigger losses during the 2000–02 bear market. Over a grueling 31-month stretch, the Nasdaq Composite Index—widely viewed as a yardstick for tech stock performance—fell a jaw-dropping 78 percent. It wasn't until 2015 that the Nasdaq Composite returned to its March 2000 peak (and, as of early 2016, it was once again below that level). In effect, back in the late 1990s, tech stock investors played the investment equivalent of Russian roulette—and those who failed to get out in time ended up surrendering 15 years of their financial life.

LOSING OUR LUNCH

A few pages back, I mentioned that we face three distinct risks when we invest. We've already talked about the risk that markets will generate terrible results, and also the risk that our investments will fare far worse than the market averages. Now, we turn to the third and final risk: the risk that we buy and sell at the wrong time.

At issue here is the enemy in the mirror. How much investment risk can we stomach? The answer we give during booming markets is often quite different from our answer when the market is down 50 percent, our neighbors are in despair and the pundits are declaring that there is worse to come. As George Goodman, under the pseudonym Adam Smith, wrote in his 1968 bestseller *The Money Game*, "If you don't know who you are, this [the stock market] is an expensive place to find out."

If we are going to sell stocks in a panic, it's much better to do so when share prices are close to their all-time high, rather than waiting until stocks are down sharply. How can we figure out how much risk we can tolerate, so we sell during good times rather than at a market bottom? There is, unfortunately, no stock market simulator that can hammer home the sense of terror that many feel at times of market turmoil. But you might probe the issue from a few different angles.

For starters, if you were investing in 2008 and 2009, check whether you bought, sold or sat tight. Our memories are often unreliable, so dig up your old account statements and take a close look at the trades you made. While our investment savvy should improve over time, we shouldn't fool ourselves: Probably the best indicator of how we will behave in the next bear market is how we behaved the last time around.

What if you haven't lived through a major bear market? Imagine the stock market fell 50 percent. Try thinking about the consequences in terms of raw dollars lost. Let's say you have $500,000 in savings, including $400,000 in stocks. Suddenly, your $500,000 portfolio is worth $300,000. The money is gone and, for all you know, it isn't coming back. Indeed, there is every chance your $300,000 could soon be worth $250,000 or even less. How would you feel—and how would you react?

Often, we own a portfolio we aren't entirely happy with, because a host of mental mistakes leaves us anchored to our current holdings. To get yourself unstuck, you might try this question: "If a neighbor, who is the same age and has similar financial circumstances, asked me for financial advice, what portfolio would I recommend?" If the portfolio you would suggest to your hypothetical neighbor is different from the one you currently own, you should ask yourself why.

Alternatively, to get at the same issue, you might ask this question: "If I were starting from scratch, would I buy the portfolio I own today?"

Even if you ask yourself the above two questions and affirm that you are happy with your current portfolio, you should wrestle with one final question: "Am I taking more risk than is necessary?"

If we have amassed enough money to lead the life we want, we have won the game. Why would we keep playing—and risk throwing away the financial security we have achieved? We might be comfortable keeping 70 percent of our portfolio in stocks. But if we have amassed sufficient savings that we don't need great investment returns, it might make sense to throttle back our stock exposure to 40 or 50 percent. The odds are, we will leave less money to our heirs. But there's also less chance that we will die broke.

FINAL THOUGHTS

M y paternal grandfather, whom everybody called Clem, was born in 1905 in working-class London. His mother died when he was young and he was raised by an aunt who served plenty of food to her own children, while putting far less on the plates intended for Clem and his sister, Connie. He left school at age 12 and joined the post office, where he sorted mail. Thanks to a stint at night school, Clem landed a clerical job in the Civil Service. He worked there for the rest of his life. Eventually, he came to enjoy the comforts of the middle class, including owning a home and a car, though it wasn't until his 70s that he bothered with a telephone. Both of his children—my father and my aunt—went to Cambridge University, at a time when relatively few students were admitted from state schools in the north of England.

In almost every election, Clem voted for the Labour Party and he considered himself a socialist. He understood, better than most, that poverty was a breeding ground for all kinds of social ills. But he would often add, with a slight tilt of his head for emphasis, that "if anybody should have grown up to be a criminal, it was me." Clem's message: Poverty may explain crime. But it doesn't excuse the behavior of any one individual.

The same applies to managing money.

There are all kinds of explanations for why we're so poor at handling our finances. We can blame our hardwired instincts, conventional wisdom, Wall Street's greed and corporate America's relentless marketing. But while I can understand why people go astray, my sympathy is in shorter supply. In the end, nobody sticks a gun to our head and forces us to spend too much and buy overpriced investment products. We all still have a choice—and we should be especially careful with our financial decisions, because the stakes are so high. Make the wrong choices, and our lives could be dogged by financial worries. Make the right choices, and we could have the financial freedom to lead the life we want.

This book is about *How to Think About Money*. Did I convince you? Maybe you are still inclined to try your hand at beating the market. Perhaps you can't help but want the fancy new sports car. Maybe you're sufficiently uncertain about your life expectancy that you can't bring yourself to delay claiming Social

Security. Still, with any luck, you have found the preceding chapters provocative and you are taking a fresh look at your finances.

Now that I've got you thinking, it is time for some doing. For those readers who were distracted along the way by their children or their iPhones, and can't recall every word of this book, here is a brief recap—in the form of 12 suggestions for getting the most out of your money:

1. We favor possessions for their lasting value, but often we get greater happiness when we spend our money on experiences. Forget the new car. Instead, travel across Europe.

2. We should use our dollars to create special times with friends and family. Take the kids to a sports event and your spouse to the theater. Have dinner out with friends. Fly across the country to see the grandchildren.

3. We should design a life for ourselves where we can spend our days doing what we love. To that end, we should save every penny we can early in our adult life, so we quickly buy ourselves some financial freedom. In our 40s or 50s, we might use that freedom to switch into a career that's perhaps less lucrative, but which we may find more fulfilling.

4. We should worry less about dying early in retirement, and more about living longer than we ever imagined. Faced with that risk, most of us should delay Social Security to get a larger monthly check, and also consider buying longevity insurance and immediate fixed annuities that pay lifetime income.

5. Our investment time horizon is measured not in months and years, but in decades and decades. We should strive to look beyond the market's short-term turmoil and instead aim to collect the staggering gains that can accrue to those who hold diversified stock portfolios for 30 or even 50 years. Indeed, while a long bear market can impoverish retirees who don't have enough in bonds and cash investments, it can be a great gift to young adults who are good savers, because it offers the chance to buy stocks at bargain prices.

6. We should hold down our fixed monthly costs, such as the sum we devote to mortgage or rent, cars, utilities, groceries and insurance premiums. Those low fixed costs will give us more financial breathing room, which can ease our sense of financial stress, leave us with more money for discretionary "fun" spending—and allow us to save voraciously.

7. Good savings habits don't come naturally, so we need to make salting away money as painless as possible. That means signing up for payroll contributions to our 401(k) plan and setting up automatic investment plans, where money is pulled from our bank account each month and invested directly into the mutual funds we choose. It also means adopting easy-to-follow financial rules, such as always adding $100 to the monthly mortgage check and always saving financial windfalls, including tax refunds and income from a second job.

8. The harder we try to beat the market, the more likely we are to fail, thanks to the hefty investment

costs we incur. To avoid that fate, we should stop trying to outsmart other investors and instead embrace humility—in the guise of a globally diversified portfolio of low-cost index funds.

9. We should never forget that stocks have fundamental value. For a diversified stock portfolio, that fundamental value will change much more slowly than market prices. To keep ourselves grounded, we should focus on the dividends and earnings we buy with every dollar invested, we should have a handle on the market's likely long-run return, and we should think like shoppers, viewing market declines with the same enthusiasm that we view a sale at the local department store.

10. Chronologically, retirement might be our life's final financial goal, but we should put it first. Retirement is the most expensive of our goals, and hence we need to save and collect investment gains for many decades to amass enough money. Retirement is also distinctly different from other goals, like buying a home or paying for our children's college education. What's different? Retirement won't be optional for most of us and we can't expect to pay for it out of our paycheck, because at that point we won't have one.

11. We should take a broad view of our finances—and the unifying notion should be the income from our human capital, or the lack thereof. The paychecks we collect over our lifetime are like a bond that generates 40 years of fairly steady income. That income stream can diversify a portfolio that's heavily invested in stocks, provide the savings we need to set aside for retirement, and allow us to

take on debt early in our adult life and then repay it by the time we retire. We also need to protect our human capital, by ensuring we have adequate health, disability and life insurance.

12. The goal isn't to get rich. Rather, the goal is to have enough money to lead the life we want. We shouldn't put that at risk by incurring excessive investment costs, straying too far from a global indexing strategy and failing to buy insurance against major financial risks.

None of this is especially complicated or clever. But putting these ideas into practice takes thought and effort. We need to ignore our instincts, rein in our emotions, take a deep breath and focus relentlessly on what's best for us—for our happiness and our financial freedom over a lifetime that might span nine decades.

Sound like a lot of work? It's nothing compared to the potential reward. With a sense of mission and the simple steps outlined above, it is amazing how much wealth we can amass—and how much happier our financial life can be.

ABOUT THE
AUTHOR

Jonathan Clements is a financial writer living just north of New York City. Born in London, England, Jonathan graduated from Cambridge University. He spent almost 20 years at *The Wall Street Journal* in New York, where he was a personal-finance columnist. Jonathan also worked at Citigroup for six years as Director of Financial Education for the U.S. wealth-management business.

Jonathan has written a novel and five earlier personal-finance books, including the *Jonathan Clements Money Guide*, whose content will be available at JonathanClements.com starting early 2017. He recently joined Creative Planning, an SEC registered investment advisor, where he serves as a board member and Director of Financial Education. An avid bicyclist, Jonathan can, on many mornings, be found pedaling madly around town. He's married, with two children and two stepchildren.

You can learn more at JonathanClements.com or at the *Jonathan Clements Money Guide*'s Facebook page. You can also keep up with Jonathan's writing on Twitter @ClementsMoney. Every few months, he puts out a free newsletter. You can see past issues at JonathanClements.com and get on the distribution list by writing to Jonathan@JonathanClements.com.

NOTES

Many of the studies, articles and academic papers listed below are available free online. Simply type the title and author's name into your favorite search engine.

---

[1] For an introduction to behavioral finance, neuroeconomics, evolutionary psychology and happiness research, consider four books. For behavioral finance, try Michael M. Pompian, *Behavioral Finance and Wealth Management: How to Build Optimal Portfolios That Account for Investor Biases*, Wiley (2006). For neuroeconomics, read Jason Zweig, *Your Money and Your Brain: How the New Science of Neuroeconomics Can Help Make You Rich*, Simon & Schuster (2007). For evolutionary psychology, turn to Terry Burnham and Jay Phelan, *Mean Genes: From Sex to Money to Food: Taming Our Primal Instincts*, Perseus Publishing (2000). For more on happiness research, try Sonja Lyubomirsky, *The How of Happiness: A Scientific Approach to Getting the Life You Want*, Penguin Press (2007).

[2] I couldn't resist footnoting a sentence devoted to not footnoting.

[3] Alois Stutzer and Bruno S. Frey, "What Happiness Research Can Tell Us About Self-Control Problems and Utility Misprediction," IZA Discussion Paper No. 1952 (January 2006).

[4] Elizabeth W. Dunn, Daniel T. Gilbert and

149

Timothy D. Wilson, "If Money Doesn't Make You Happy, Then You Probably Aren't Spending It Right," *Journal of Consumer Psychology*, Vol. 21, Issue 2 (April 2011).

[5] Pew Research Center, *Are We Happy Yet?* (February 2006).

[6] Sonja Lyubomirsky, Kennon M. Sheldon and David Schkade, "Pursuing Happiness: The Architecture of Sustainable Change," *Review of General Psychology*, Vol. 9, No. 2 (2005).

[7] Pew Research Center, *People in Emerging Markets Catch Up to Advanced Economies in Life Satisfaction* (October 2014).

[8] Sonja Lyubomirsky, Kennon M. Sheldon and David Schkade, "Pursuing Happiness: The Architecture of Sustainable Change," *Review of General Psychology*, Vol. 9, No. 2 (2005).

[9] Daniel Kahneman and Angus Deaton, "High Income Improves Evaluation of Life But Not Emotional Well-Being," *Proceedings of the National Academy of Sciences*, Vol. 107, No. 38 (Sept. 21, 2010).

[10] Daniel Kahneman, Alan B. Krueger, David Schkade, Norbert Schwarz and Arthur A. Stone, "Would You Be Happier If You Were Richer? A Focusing Illusion," *Science*, Vol. 312 (June 2006).

[11] Daniel Kahneman and Angus Deaton, "High Income Improves Evaluation of Life But Not Emotional Well-Being," *Proceedings of the National Academy of Sciences*, Vol. 107, No. 38 (Sept. 21, 2010).

[12] David Schkade and Daniel Kahneman, "Does Living in California Make People Happy?" *Psychological Science*, Vol. 9, No. 5 (September 1998).

[13] Erzo F.P. Luttmer, "Neighbors as Negatives: Relative Earnings and Well-Being," *Quarterly Journal of*

Economics (August 2005).

[14] John Gathergood, "Debt and Depression: Causal Links and Social Norm Effects," *The Economic Journal* (September 2012).

[15] Daniel Kahneman, Alan B. Krueger, David Schkade, Norbert Schwarz and Arthur Stone, "Toward National Well-Being Accounts," *AEA Papers and Proceedings* (May 2004)

[16] HuffingtonPost.com, "Divorce Study Shows That Couples With Longer Commutes Are More Likely to Divorce" (Aug. 13, 2013).

[17] Leaf Van Boven and Thomas Gilovich, "To Do or to Have? That Is the Question," *Journal of Personality and Social Psychology*, Vol. 85, No. 6 (2003).

[18] Kim Parker, *Parenthood and Happiness: It's More Complicated Than You Think*, Pew Research Center (Feb. 7, 2014).

[19] Chris M. Herbst and John Ifcher, "The Increasing Happiness of Parents," *Review of Economics of the Household* (July 2015).

[20] Angus Deaton and Arthur A. Stone, "Evaluative and Hedonic Wellbeing Among Those With and Without Children at Home," *Proceedings of the National Academy of Sciences*, Vol. 111, No. 4 (Jan. 28, 2014).

[21] Elizabeth W. Dunn, Daniel T. Gilbert and Timothy D. Wilson, "If Money Doesn't Make You Happy, Then You Probably Aren't Spending It Right," *Journal of Consumer Psychology*, Vol. 21, Issue 2 (April 2011).

[22] Richard M. Ryan and Edward L. Deci, "Self-Determination Theory and the Facilitation of Intrinsic Motivation, Social Development, and Well-Being," *American Psychologist*, Vol. 55, No. 1 (January 2000).

[23] I was tempted to put in a plug for the *Jonathan*

Clements Money Guide, but decided it might be considered tacky.

[24] Daniel Kahneman, Alan B. Krueger, David Schkade, Norbert Schwarz and Arthur Stone, "Toward National Well-Being Accounts," *AEA Papers and Proceedings* (May 2004).

[25] Julianne Holt-Lunstad, Timothy B. Smith and J. Bradley Layton, "Social Relationships and Mortality Risk: A Meta-Analytic Review," *PLOS Medicine* (July 27, 2010). PLOS is an acronym for Public Library of Science.

[26] Note to quibblers: We're only counting Grover Cleveland once, though he did serve two nonconsecutive terms. As of mid-2016, there have been 44 U.S. presidencies, but only 43 presidents.

[27] Felicitie C. Bell and Michael L. Miller, *Life Tables for the United States Social Security Area 1900–2100*, Social Security Administration, Office of the Chief Actuary, Actuarial Study No. 120 (August 2005). The figures used here, which are from table 11, are cohort life expectancies. Cohort life expectancies reflect actual or expected declines in mortality rates. By contrast, period life expectancies reflect the mortality rate at every age as of the year in question, without accounting for any actual or expected improvements. For instance, for someone born in 2000, the period life expectancy was 74 years for men and 79 years for women. The cohort life expectancy was 80 years for men and 84 years for women. The latter estimates are a better guide to how long you might live.

[28] For this insight and these figures, my thanks go to financial planner Bob Frey and actuary Joe Tomlinson.

[29] Social Security's *2015 OASDI Trustees Report*, Supplemental Single-Year Tables, Table V.A2.

[30] While most workers plan to retire at age 65, they typically end up retiring even earlier, at age 62, according to the Employee Benefit Research Institute's *2016 Retirement Confidence Survey.*

[31] For more about the conundrum created by our aging population, see Robert D. Arnott and Anne Casscells, "Demographics and Capital Market Returns," *Financial Analysts Journal* (March/April 2003).

[32] David G. Blanchflower and Andrew J. Oswald, "Is Well-Being U-Shaped Over the Life Cycle?" *Social Science & Medicine* 66 (2008).

[33] For a good summary of the literature on age and motivation, see Gottfried Catania and Raymond Randall, "The Relationship Between Age and Intrinsic and Extrinsic Motivation in Workers in a Maltese Cultural Context," *International Journal of Arts and Sciences*, Vol. 6, No. 2 (2013).

[34] Lauren L. Schmitz, "Do Working Conditions at Older Ages Shape the Health Gradient?" Working paper (September 2015).

[35] American Institute for Economic Research, *New Careers for Older Workers* (2015).

[36] Mihaly Csikszentmihalyi, *Flow: The Psychology of Optimal Experience*, Harper & Row (1990).

[37] Jonathan Clements, "Three Questions That Can Change Your Finances . . . and Your Life," *The Wall Street Journal* (Feb. 27, 2015).

[38] Anna Prior, "Route to an $8 Million Portfolio Started With Frugal Living," *The Wall Street Journal* (March 19, 2015).

[39] These price-earnings multiples are based on reported earnings through Dec. 31, 1915, and Dec. 31, 2015. At the time, investors would have thought the

P/E was slightly different, because full-year earnings hadn't yet been reported.

[40] You can find MSCI data at https://www.msci.com/end-of-day-data-search. To do a customized performance search, click on the name of the index.

[41] John C. Bogle and Michael W. Nolan Jr., "Occam's Razor Redux: Establishing Reasonable Expectations for Financial Market Returns," *Journal of Portfolio Management* (Fall 2015).

[42] William J. Bernstein and Robert D. Arnott, "Earnings Growth: The Two Percent Dilution," *Financial Analysts Journal* (September/October 2003). In the years since the study appeared, share buybacks have roughly matched share issuance, though it isn't clear whether this is a short-term phenomenon or long-term trend.

[43] John Maynard Keynes, *The General Theory of Employment, Interest and Money*, Macmillan Press (1936).

[44] While an alarming number of Social Security recipients claim benefits at age 62, there are signs of smarter financial behavior, as detailed in Alicia H. Munnell and Anqi Chen, *Trends in Social Security Claiming*, Center for Retirement Research at Boston College (May 2015).

[45] For more, see Michael M. Pompian, *Behavioral Finance and Wealth Management: How to Build Optimal Portfolios That Account for Investor Biases*, Wiley (2006).

[46] Meir Statman, "How Your Emotions Get in the Way of Smart Investing," *The Wall Street Journal* (June 14, 2015).

[47] Thomas J. Stanley and William D. Danko, *The Millionaire Next Door: The Surprising Secrets of America's Wealthy*, Longstreet Press (1996).

[48] Thomas J. Stanley, *Stop Acting Rich . . . And Start Living Like a Real Millionaire,* Wiley (2009).

[49] When I give speeches, I will often read this list of statistics and then pronounce, "As I like to tell people, when you meet a millionaire, you'll know him by his bad haircut—and his terrible hangover."

[50] Jonathan Clements, "Compare and Contrast: Bear Market of 1973–74 Changed How People Judged Investment Performance," *The Wall Street Journal* (May 28, 1996).

[51] Michael C. Jensen, "The Performance of Mutual Funds in the Period 1945–64," *Journal of Finance*, Vol. 23, Issue 2 (1968).

[52] Aye M. Soe, *SPIVA U.S. Scorecard,* S&P Dow Jones Indices, McGraw Hill Financial, Report 1 (Year-End 2015).

[53] Aye M. Soe, *Does Past Performance Matter? The Persistence Scorecard,* S&P Dow Jones Indices, McGraw Hill Financial, Exhibit 5 (January 2016).

[54] Benjamin Graham, *The Intelligent Investor,* HarperCollins (1949).

[55] To find the current price-earnings ratio and dividend yield for the S&P 500, go to WSJmarkets.com and click on the "U.S. Stocks" tab. Look for the link labeled "P/Es and Yields on Major Indexes."

[56] For the current Shiller P/E, as well as historical information on dividends and earnings, find the homepage for Robert J. Shiller, click on the "Online Data" tab and then open the spreadsheet labeled "U.S. Stock Markets 1871-Present and CAPE Ratio."

[57] For instance, see Adam Smith, *The Wealth of Nations,* Book II, Chapter 1 (1776). Zvi Bodie, Robert C. Merton and William F. Samuelson, "Labor Supply Flexibility and Portfolio Choice in a Life Cycle Model, "

Journal of Economic Dynamics and Control (1992). Roger G. Ibbotson, Kevin X. Zhu, Peng Chen and Moshe A. Milevsky, *Lifetime Financial Advice: Human Capital, Asset Allocation and Insurance*, CFA Institute Research Foundation (2007).

The 70 percent figure comes from Tiffany Julian, *Work-Life Earnings by Field of Degree and Occupation for People With a Bachelor's Degree: 2011*, American Community Survey Briefs, U.S. Census Bureau (October 2012). The study puts average projected lifetime earnings at $1.4 million for high school graduates, $2.4 million for those with a bachelor's degree, $2.8 million for those with a master's, $4.2 million for those with a professional degree and $3.5 million for those with a doctorate.

[58] Among financial planners, the 4 percent withdrawal rate has become a fairly standard recommendation, thanks in part to the pioneering work of William P. Bengen, "Determining Withdrawal Rates Using Historical Data," *Journal of Financial Planning* (October 1994). The assumption is that retirees will withdraw 4 percent of their nest egg's value in the first year of retirement. In subsequent years, they step up the dollar amount withdrawn with inflation. Taxes will likely be owed on this money, and any dividends and interest received count toward that year's total allowable withdrawal.

[59] Chenkai Wu, Michelle C. Odden, Gwenith G. Fisher and Robert S. Stawski, "Association of Retirement Age with Mortality: A Population-Based Longitudinal Study Among Older Adults in the USA," *Journal of Epidemiology and Community Health* (March 21, 2016).

[60] There's an extensive literature on time

diversification. You can find a summary of the debate in Donald G. Bennyhoff, *Time Diversification and Horizon-Based Asset Allocations*, Vanguard Investment Counseling & Research (2008).

[61] John C. Bogle, "The Arithmetic of 'All-In' Investment Expenses," *Financial Analysts Journal*, Vol. 70, No. 1 (January/February 2014). Included in Bogle's 2.27 percent total annual cost for actively managed funds is 0.5 percent for the sales charge levied by some—but not all—actively managed funds.

[62] Brad M. Barber and Terrance Odean, "The Behavior of Individual Investors," SSRN.com (September 2011).

[63] My thanks to William Bernstein for mentioning the relevance of Pascal's wager to finance often enough that the author eventually got it.

[64] Ronald Doeswijk, Trevin Lam and Laurens Swinkels, "The Global Multi-Asset Market Portfolio, 1959–2012," *Financial Analysts Journal*, Vol. 70, No. 2 (March/April 2014). While this investment mix reflects the "market portfolio" or "investable universe," it isn't representative of global wealth. To get a handle on global wealth, you need to add items such as residential real estate, the value of private businesses, government-owned assets, precious metals, art and— if you want to get really fancy—the value of our human capital.

That brings us to an intriguing question: If we're interested in global wealth, rather than in what the investable universe looks like, should we even include bonds? For every dollar lent, there is a dollar that has been borrowed, so the world's net bond position is zero. If we were to wave a magic wand and eliminate all corporate, mortgage and government bonds, we would enrich shareholders by boosting the value of stocks, enrich homeowners by increasing their home equity and help taxpayers by trimming the interest payments that they fund with their tax dollars. But, by an equal sum, we would also impoverish holders of corporate, mortgage and government bonds.

[65] FolioInvesting.com offers a "ready-to-go" portfolio of 15 exchange-traded index funds called the CWM Global Market folio, which aims to replicate the market portfolio.